HOW TO MAKE A QUILT

25 Easy Lessons For Beginners

Bonnie Leman

and

Louise O. Townsend

Moon Over The Mountain Publishing Co.
6700 W. 44th Ave., Wheatridge, Colo. 80033

ACKNOWLEDGMENTS

Thanks to Judy Martin and Marie Shirer for their editorial comments and suggestions, to Mary Leman Austin and Kathy Dubois Reed for their production assistance, to Theresa Eisinger, Laurie Meador, and Marla Gibbs Stefanelli for their illustrations.

ON THE COVER: Daisy Chain, 80″ x 95″, pieced and hand quilted by Mrs. Robert M. Brown of Greeley, Colorado, in 1982. This pattern was designed by Judy Martin for the premiere issue of *QUILTMAKER* magazine (Spring/Summer 1982). Its two simple blocks make it a design reminiscent of the old-time Wedding Ring patterns. A pattern for this quilt may be found on page 88. Photograph by Jerry DeFelice.

TABLE OF CONTENTS

Introduction 6
1. What Kind of Pattern Should You Choose
   for Your First Quilt? 7
2. Setting Arrangements and Borders 11
3. Choosing Colors 14
4. Estimating Yardage 17
5. Choosing and Preparing Fabrics 20
6. Choosing Fillers and Linings 23
7. Choosing Threads and Other Sewing Supplies 26
8. How to Make Templates for Piecing and Appliqué 29
9. How to Mark and Cut for Hand or Machine Piecing 32
10. How to Mark and Cut for Hand or Machine Appliqué . . . 35
11. How to Hand Piece 38
12. How to Machine Piece 41
13. How to Hand Appliqué 43
14. How to Machine Appliqué 46
15. Blocking and Pressing 48
16. How to Set Blocks Together 50
17. How to Miter Borders 57
18. Choosing a Quilting Pattern 61
19. Marking a Quilting Pattern 64
20. Basting the Quilt Layers 67
21. Using a Hoop or a Frame 70
22. How to Quilt 72
23. Binding the Quilt 78
24. Signing Your Quilt 82
25. Caring for Your Quilt 84
    Suggested Reading 87
    Pattern for Cover Quilt (Daisy Chain) 88

INTRODUCTION

One of the readers' favorite features in *Quilter's Newsletter Magazine* has been its monthly quiltmaking lessons. Although these lessons were written with the beginner in mind, many experienced quilters have found useful information in them and have used them as a quick review each month. Beginners have been especially grateful that the lessons are written in an easy-to-follow style that explains how to make a quilt step-by-step. The original Easy Lessons for Beginners appeared in *QNM* issues 7-33 in the early 1970s. In 1971 we reprinted them in book form to take a quiltmaker from the very beginning of planning a quilt through the final steps of finishing it.

Those first 25 Easy Lessons were followed by other more advanced lessons, which became the basis for our book, *Patchwork Sampler Legacy Quilt: Intermediate and Advanced Lessons in Patchwork.* Other lessons followed with information on machine work, special pattern-drafting techniques, and a lengthy series on setting arrangements.

In 1984 the magazine began a new series of lessons for beginners to welcome a whole new generation of beginning quiltmakers. Not only were there many new quilters wanting to learn how to make a quilt, but also many of the methods we used in the early '70s have since been refined and improved, and new tools of the trade have been developed to make quiltmaking easier and even more fun. This revised edition of *How To Make a Quilt: 25 Easy Lessons For Beginners* is expanded from the newer lessons. More drawings and special instructions have been added to make this the most complete guide you'll ever need for making your first quilt.

We suggest that you read the book all the way through to get an idea of the entire process of quiltmaking. Then go back to Lesson 1 and complete the steps described in each lesson. Make your first quilt a simple one, follow the directions in each lesson, and you will have an heirloom that will give enjoyment for years to come.

Bonnie Leman, Editor in Chief
Louise O. Townsend, Managing Editor
Quilter's Newsletter Magazine

Lesson No. 1: What Kind of Pattern Should You Choose for Your First Quilt?

A first quilt is a very special quilt. It introduces you to the wonderful world of quiltmaking where you will find many unexpected pleasures and satisfactions. It gives you a great feeling of accomplishment when you take that last stitch to know that you have produced something with your own hands and heart that is both useful and beautiful. And it offers a benchmark from which you can record your progress in future years. Every quilter looks back fondly at a first quilt—often in surprise at how beautifully it turned out for the work of a beginner.

There are many pretty quilt designs that will give the beginning quiltmaker a chance to learn new skills. But, how do you choose? Let's look at some of the things that can make a difference in whether you enjoy making your first quilt or you find it such a chore that you give up before finishing it. If you choose wisely, you'll enjoy the first quilt and many more to come.

Machine Work vs. Handwork. Part of the choice will depend upon the sewing skills that you already have. At this point you shouldn't have any preconceived notions about machine work versus handwork. Either is okay, if it is what *you* like to do. If you have used a sewing machine and feel comfortable making clothing or other household items, why not piece a quilt on the machine too? You'll find that the piecing goes more quickly and can be done just as precisely as handwork. If you already use your machine to do embroidery on clothing or in other craft projects, you'll find machine applique a breeze.

On the other hand, if you don't have a sewing machine, or if you are looking for handwork that you can do while waiting in the doctor's office or when you wish to relax, you'll think that hand piecing or hand appliquéing is just right. You can perfect your skills by either method with a bit of perseverance.

Size. The size of the quilt can also influence how much you enjoy your first quilting project. Your feeling of accomplishment can be enjoyed much sooner if you can see a finished product quickly, so this is not the time to begin a quilt for a king-size bed. Perhaps you'll choose to make a wall quilt because it can be as small as you wish, and you will see results right away to give you positive feelings. Some quilters start out with a patchwork block or two and make them into pillows, or combine them into a sampler quilt that can be used as a reference later on when doing other projects. If you do choose to make a bed quilt, try to make it a moderate-size one with a reasonable number of pieces. You don't want to bite off more than you can comfortably chew the first time and get discouraged about the whole experience.

Piecing vs. Appliqué. One of the choices that you'll need to make is whether to try an appliqué pattern or a pieced one. In appliqué, you sew (or *apply)* patches on top of a background fabric. In piecing, you sew patches side by side. Appliqués tend to portray something realistic such as a flower or bird, while the geometric shapes in many pieced patterns combine to give more abstract designs. To help you decide which kind of quilt design to try, leaf through a few quilt pattern books or magazines to see which kind of design appeals the most to you.

If you choose to do an appliqué design, try to find a pattern that has gentle curves. Even the experts find sharply indented flower petals difficult because there is almost no seam allowance to turn under. And they have just as much difficulty with sharply pointed leaves because there is so much fabric under the point. Very small circles (such as those used to portray cherries or grapes) are also in the difficult category and should be saved for a more advanced project. Going to the opposite extreme, appliquéing a piece with a perfectly straight side or an exact right angle is also hard to do well because it must be done so precisely. Choosing a design that has just a few, relatively large, gently curved shapes will probably work best for your first appliqué project. An example of a good pattern to try is the traditional Basket Appliqué rather than the more difficult Sadie's Choice Rose.

THIS   NOT THIS   THIS   NOT THIS

Gentle curves are easier to appliqué than sharp points.

Basket Appliqué, EASY appliqué with gentle curves and broad points.

Sadie's Choice Rose, DIFFICULT appliqué with deep curves and sharp points.

When you choose a pieced pattern for your first quilt, the size and shape of the patches can affect how much you enjoy the project. Unless you have done intricate needlework before, you'll probably find that patches that are about 2″ to 5″ per side are the best for a beginner. You don't want to work with anything too small that will require dexterity and control you don't yet have (but will gain as you practice the quilting art). At the same time, patches shouldn't be so large and ungainly that a pretty design is impossible to create. A block approximately 12″ in size with about 15 to 30 patches will be a wise choice. A good pattern for a beginning quilter might be Jacob's Ladder with 28 pieces, rather than the much more complex Feathered Star. Setting thirty Jacob's Ladder blocks together in six rows of five blocks and adding a couple of coordinating borders to enlarge the size will make a pretty and easily accomplished first bed quilt. If you are really intrigued by a pattern like Feathered Star, which has more patches in it, you might consider making just one block, or perhaps four set together with borders to create a pretty wall quilt for a first project. Then you won't get bogged down with a ponderous number of patches necessary for a larger quilt using a difficult pattern.

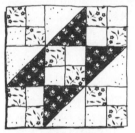

Jacob's Ladder, EASY piecing with few patches and straight seams.

Feathered Star, DIF-FICULT piecing with many patches and angled seams.

Other Considerations. The shapes of the quilt patches are important, too. Making a quilt from plain squares is not very exciting for a first project because you will want to work on something special enough to enjoy making it. Besides, many other shapes are just as easy as squares and will make the visual effect much more interesting. Here are some general guidelines to think about when looking at the shapes in a quilt pattern.

Curved seams are more difficult than straight ones, so you should avoid any but the very gentlest of curves in the patches of your first quilt. Bias fabric edges also require special handling, so you should choose patches without too many odd angles—so that no more than one side per patch has to be cut on the bias if possible.

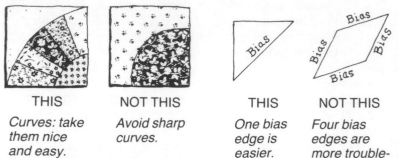

THIS	NOT THIS	THIS	NOT THIS
Curves: take them nice and easy.	Avoid sharp curves.	One bias edge is easier.	Four bias edges are more trouble-some.

Quilt patterns that have many points meeting are also a bit more difficult to execute, and may be a better choice for a second or third quilt once you get more accustomed to sewing patchwork. Angled patches—ones that require insertion with an angled seam rather than a straight one—are also more difficult to tackle, especially on the sewing machine, so try to avoid them, too.

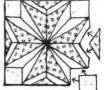

THIS	NOT THIS	THIS	NOT THIS
No sharp points make this easy.	Avoid many points meeting at one spot.	Straight seams are easily sewn.	Avoid angled patches to insert.

Love It or Leave It. We've mentioned a lot of dos and don'ts in this first beginner's lesson. But there is one consideration that should override all others when you choose a pattern for your first quilt. *You must like the design that you have chosen.* If you let too many "practical" suggestions come between you and a pattern that you really like, you'll struggle through every phase of making your first quilt, and it won't be the pleasurable experience that it should be. If the pattern that you like best has one or two "difficult" problems, consider them a challenge, and teach yourself how to overcome them. Then you'll like your quilt while you're working on it; you'll like the finished product; and, best of all, you'll like yourself for facing—and conquering—a new challenge. Welcome to the wonderful world of quilting!

Lesson No. 2: Setting Arrangements and Borders

Choosing a setting and border for your first quilt is very important—just as important to a successful quilt as the choice of a block pattern. A pretty design may get lost if you add too many other elements such as sashing (strips between blocks) or an elaborate border. But you might make the same design come alive with a simple set. Blocks set side by side may create other secondary designs that improve on the original. Perhaps just four large blocks pointing out from the center will create a spectacular quilt.

Setting Variations. Most traditional quilts are made from square blocks. The design blocks may be set side by side, or they may be alternated with plain ones in which fancy quilting is done. With alternate plain blocks, the setting will be symmetrical and pleasing if an odd number of blocks makes up each row, and if there is an odd number of rows. The blocks may also be set on the diagonal. A diagonal setting requires triangles (or half and quarter blocks) to fill in the outside edges of the quilt. Another setting option is to use sashes (sometimes called lattice strips) from 1" to 4" in width between blocks. Sashes may be added for many reasons: they can add color to the overall design or tie it all together; they can separate and define busy-looking blocks or eliminate the need to match seams on adjacent blocks; they can increase the dimensions of the quilt to a larger size; and they may offer space for decorative quilting.

Straight set (Shoo Fly)— blocks set side by side.

Straight set—alternate plain blocks.

The Quilt in its Environment. When you have found a quilt pattern that you want to try, and it is time to decide on a setting, think about how you will use the finished quilt. For example, what specific bed will the quilt adorn? In general, the design area should cover the whole top surface of a bed with borders or a continuation of the design falling down the sides of the bed. Perhaps each half of the quilt should face in toward the center, if the bed is always viewed from the side rather than the bottom. Possibly the borders will need to be extra wide if the bed is a high one. It may be necessary to round the bottom corners so they don't trail on the floor, or you might need to cut out the two lower corners to accommodate a four-poster bed.

If you are planning to hang your quilt on the wall, your only consideration will be the overall impact of the design. Wall quilts are generally smaller than bed quilts, and they often have framing borders. A single, large block, or four blocks set together, or an appliquéd "picture" design may be more appropriate hanging on the wall than lying on a bed.

Borders. Borders may vary from a narrow binding around the edge of the quilt to a series of plain, pieced, or appliquéd borders. They should enhance the beauty of the quilt and act as a frame for it, harmonizing with, not overpowering, the rest of the quilt. Design elements (perhaps a block or just part of a block) or particularly striking fabrics already used in the quilt center will help to unify the border area with the central design. This will keep it from looking like an afterthought that was just tacked onto the quilt.

Diagonal set.

Straight set with sashing.

Borders whose main function is simply to frame the design often look best if they are darker or brighter than the central area. An easy way to create a border is just to change the coloring of the outside row of blocks. You can also add one or more borders (either solid or printed fabrics) to the quilt top. Quilts that use butted seams within the quilt blocks (such as a Log Cabin design) look fine with butted borders, while most other designs appear more symmetrically framed with mitered borders. You should make this decision in the planning stage, because it may affect the yardage needed. (Subsequent lessons discuss both yardage and mitering.)

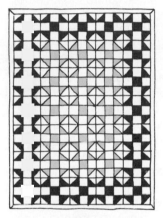

Pieced border—same blocks with darker coloring.

Plain borders (mitered corners).

Additional Tips. To help you decide on a setting for your quilt, study photos in books or magazines to choose what appeals most to you. Then, when planning the setting for your first quilt (or any quilt), use paper and pencil before cutting anything out. First, sketch the general idea that you have; then add or subtract elements to see which set looks best. Perhaps sashing should be added—but if it looks terrible with your chosen pattern, you might enlarge the block size so that sashing isn't needed. Maybe a wide, dark border is needed to frame the design, or maybe the design looks best going right out to the edge of the quilt with a simple binding. You'll never know until you try it out, and it is much easier to plan on paper first than to sit down and cut out patches and piece them together into a quilt top that doesn't look right. If you make your setting plans first and choose them wisely, the cutting, piecing, and quilting will be much more enjoyable because you'll know that the finished quilt will be a beauty!

Lesson No. 3: Choosing Colors

The colors that you choose and the way you arrange them will help to make your first quilt unique and different from all others. Since taste in colors is highly individual, you'll want to think carefully about choosing these colors. One of your most important considerations is that you pick a color scheme that pleases you. You will do your best work and look forward eagerly to the finished product if you use colors that you truly like.

Colors from Your Wardrobe or Home. But how do you decide what colors you like best? Or which colors "go together"? Though you may feel unconfident about making these choices, remember that you already know how to put colors together in a pleasing manner. Think about the colors that you enjoy wearing. What colors are the accessories that you wear with them—the jewelry, or belt, or shoes and handbag that give the whole outfit pizzazz? Or, think about the colors that you have used to decorate your home. Are there rooms that have two sharply contrasting colors, such as a blue and white kitchen? Or do you tend more toward combining several blending colors in a favorite room? Is there a one- or two-color room that has a splash of bright color in pillows, or a vase, or an area rug? You can try any of these color combinations for your first quilt—if they work together in your outfits or your favorite room, they'll surely please you in a quilt.

Colors from Magazines. If you are still unsure about making choices, try leafing through several decorator or fashion magazines to find color combinations that you like. Many quilters keep a file folder of pictures that appeal to them colorwise so that they'll have something to work from the next time they start a quilt. You can add to such a file by collecting postcards of paintings or other artwork that appeals to you.

Colors from Nature. Another way to collect color combinations that you like is to observe nature. The next time you're out for a walk or a ride in the car, take along a pencil and paper, and write down all of the colors that you see at one of your favorite spots, or when there is an especially pretty sunset, or a wonderfully misty morning fog. When making your list, note which colors predominate—the ones that really stand out from the rest because they are rich and deep, or because they take up a large part of the scene. You'll see many shades of green if you are looking at the woods, or lots of bold blue sky if you're out on the plains. Notice which colors add an unexpected dash of sparkle—just small amounts of color, but ones that really stand out. Perhaps it will be bright red tulips on a stony gray ledge, or a twinkle of sunny yellow highlights on deep blue water. Notice which colors seem to recede or move into the background. These are probably the so-called "cool" colors of blue, green, or purple, or they are darker shades of any color. Which colors come forward or seem to be closest to you? They are usually the "warm" colors of red, orange, or yellow, or they are the lighter shades of any color. A list of colors that "go together" in a natural setting can easily translate into a pretty color combination for a quilt.

Colors from Fabric. If you still haven't come up with a color or group of colors that you really like, make a visit to a local fabric shop and look for a multicolored printed fabric that really appeals to you. Make a note of the colors in the print as well as the amount of each color in relation to the others. One or two colors will probably stand out. Perhaps several shades of one color or several similar colors are used with just a dash of another color for an accent. If the fabric is suitable for quiltmaking (see Lesson Number 5 on page 20 for how to choose fabrics), you might select this print and a group of coordinating fabrics as the ones you'll use in your quilt.

Using Colors in a Pattern. Once you have found colors for your quilt it's time to combine them with the quilt pattern and setting that you have chosen. If you are working from a purchased pattern or one in a magazine, it may suggest specific colors or at least indicate which patches should be light or dark. These suggestions may work perfectly well, but don't be surprised if your own ideas will look better and more personally "yours." Put a piece of tracing paper over your quilt design, and experiment with colored pencils, colored pens, or crayons to see where you want to place each color. You can use this tracing-paper method over a quilt photograph or over a line drawing that has already been colored. Although you may not be able to exactly match the colors you have in mind, you can at least get a good idea of what the finished quilt will look like. If you are uncertain about use of color, try copying the same lights and darks as in the original color scheme. Then try several different combinations of your chosen colors. You'll be surprised how much one quilt design can change just by switching

The look of a quilt block can be changed dramatically by using different arrangements of light and dark patches.

the lights and darks or by changing the amount of each color used. Take a look at your experimental drawings, and choose one that pleases you. It's a lot easier to do this experimenting on paper than to cut out the patches from fabric and find that they don't look right after a lot of work.

How Many Colors? There really aren't any "rules" about how many colors to use in your quilt. A monochromatic color scheme—one using many shades of a single color—might become rather boring unless you have lots of contrast between the light and dark shades. You might choose one print with a little of a different color in it to add a dash of special interest. If you plan to use just two colors in your quilt, try to choose a very light and a very dark color so that the design will be sharply defined. Using a print in such a color scheme may work well if it is a very small print so that the edges of the design are not blurred; otherwise, the best choice is probably two solids. If you are using several colors, you can hold the design together by repeating the appearance of one or two of the colors in all blocks, and by repeating all of the colors at least three or four times across the surface of the quilt.

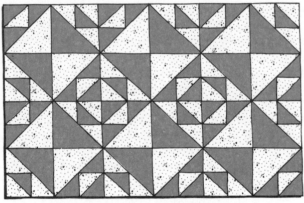

Use sharply contrasting fabrics to define the pattern in a two-fabric quilt.

Texture and Depth. Remember that the darker, richer shades of color will tend to recede and add depth to the quilt surface. They will help to define other lighter or brighter colors and make them stand out. The lightest shades will stand out the most, but if you use too many of them, the whole design may become too pale and fade away. Experiment with paper and colored pencils to seek a pleasing balance of color and contrasting lights and darks for your quilt design.

Lesson No. 4: Estimating Yardage

For your first quilt you may choose a published pattern that includes yardage requirements, and you won't have to bother with figuring the correct amount of fabric to buy. Chances are that sooner or later, though, you will want to plan your own design, and you will need to estimate how much fabric is needed for it. The correct calculations will save you time and money when you make your purchase and insure that you will have enough of every fabric to complete the quilt as you envision it.

Your Quilt Plan. In order to figure the yardage, you'll need to refer to your quilt plan on paper. From it you can make a list of how many of each pattern piece in each fabric you will need to cut. Add up the number of pieces of the same shape and fabric in one block, and multiply by the number of blocks. The quilt plan on paper will also aid you in counting the number and size of setting squares, sashes, and border strips.

Drafting Patterns. Once you have a list of all of the pieces needed for the quilt top, it is a good idea to draft a set of full-size patterns with the ¼" seam allowances (for pieced patterns) or the ³⁄₁₆" turn-under allowances (for hand appliqué patterns) included. It is important to estimate yardage with patterns that include the seam or turn-under allowance so that you can measure shapes accurately.

Unusable Fabric. When preparing fabric for cutting out the patches, you should not count on the last 2" of the width because of variance in actual fabric widths, shrinkage, and trimming off the selvedges (which are too tightly woven to sew through and may leave puckers in your work). Thus, a 44"-45" width of fabric will yield about 42" of usable yard goods.

Cutting Layouts. While figuring yardage, you will find it useful to make a cutting layout. If this is your first quilt, you may find it helpful to work with an actual length of fabric and templates. For a second or third quilt the cutting layout might be a scaled drawing on graph paper, or a freehand sketch with measurements written in. You will need a cutting layout for each fabric used in the quilt. One by one, consider the pattern pieces you have listed, starting with the longest and largest pieces first, and plan how to arrange the pieces for cutting.

Borders and Sashes. Whenever possible, long border or sashing strips should have no seams in them, so draw these long strips on the cutting layout first. Remember to add ¼" seam allowances to all sides of these pieces. Some quilters also add about 2" extra to the length of the long pieces just for insurance—in case the quilt top ends up slightly larger than expected.

Binding. If you plan to bind the edges of the quilt in fabric that matches one of the fabrics used in the quilt, you will also need to calculate this yardage before planning for cutting out smaller pieces. If you will use straight-grain binding, plan the proper width and length of fabric just as you did for long borders. You should add about 6″ extra to the length for manipulating the mitered corners. If you plan to use bias binding, a one-yard square (36″ x 36″) of fabric will make approximately 16 yards of 2″ bias binding. Buy this amount, or a little more or less, depending on the finished dimensions of your quilt and the width of binding you wish to use.

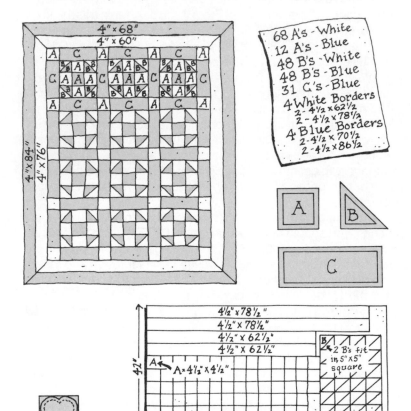

Cutting Layout for White Fabric

To make cutting layouts and figure yardage, you need a quilt plan on paper, a list of pieces needed, and templates with seam allowances. Draw appliqué shapes inside of squares or triangles to figure yardage more easily.

Figuring the Yardage. After fabric for the larger pieces has been calculated and drawn on the layout, then smaller patches might fit in the remainder, or they can be cut from an additional length of fabric. When working with appliqué shapes, you may find it useful to draw the shape (with turn-under allowance) inside a square or triangle and then figure out how many of the squares or triangles you will need. To figure how many patches of a particular shape and size can be cut across the width of the fabric, measure the width of a patch and divide it into 42" or whatever width remains after cutting all border strips. Drop the fraction, if any, and divide this number into the total number needed of this type of patch to see how many rows of patches are needed. Multiply the number of rows by the length measurement of the patch to see how much yardage is needed. After measuring for all patches required from a particular fabric, add a little extra for shrinkage and insurance.

A good general rule to follow is that the total yardage for a standard double-bed size quilt top will be approximately ten yards altogether, though you may need to buy more to cut seamless borders. Stripes, repeat designs, or large motifs on the fabric may require more yardage to make the patches match. If you are in doubt, it is wise to buy a bit more yardage than you think you'll need. Extra fabric can be saved for your next quilt.

Yardage for Lining. When figuring the lining for your quilt, you'll need a piece about 2" larger all around than the finished size of the quilt. If there are no sides of the quilt measuring about 40" or less, you'll need to buy at least two (and sometimes three) lengths of yard goods to be pieced together for the lining. The seam(s) of the lining may run either horizontally or vertically on the back (see the drawings on page 25 for some examples), so you'll want to calculate the most economical use of fabric in order to save money on your purchase. Extra fabric might be used to bind the quilt edges, or it can go into your scrapbag for future use.

Quick Estimates. To some quiltmakers saving time is more important than saving money, so they prefer to estimate a generous amount of yardage rather than take the time to figure it accurately. They believe that if any fabric is left over, they will use it eventually in another quilt—so there is no waste in the long run. If you would rather budget your time than money (or if you want to buy fabric without specific plans), you might want to follow their lead by buying one-half to one yard of every accent fabric to be used in small amounts in your quilt and three yards of every other fabric. However, if your budget won't allow you to buy more than you actually need, take the time to figure the yardage by using the method in this lesson. This will also insure that you buy enough.

Lesson No. 5: Choosing and Preparing Fabrics

Your quilt plan on paper suggests the colors that you intend to use in your first quilt, but it's quite possible that there isn't a single fabric that is the exact shade of your colored pencils, and it is quite likely that you did not draw any prints in your picture. So there will be many decisions required when you choose the actual fabrics, and your quilt drawing will act as a general guide to tell you how much fabric you'll need to collect from your sewing scrapbag, or, more likely, from the nearest quilt or fabric shop.

Using Solids. Choosing all solid colors can give a bold, contemporary look to your work, and if the design is an especially busy one with many shapes and colors, using solids may help to control it. If the perfect color is impossible to find, you might substitute a small-scale, overall print that "reads" as the color you want. We recommend that for your first quilt you try to find the colors you want in all-cotton fabric, rather than buying a blend just for its color, because some blends can be harder to work with.

Using Prints. If you prefer the "country" look, using many prints will give a quaint, traditional feeling to your work. Also, a simple design, or one in which you plan to use just a single color, will probably be enhanced if you mix solids and prints to add texture to the quilt surface. The best way to do this is to vary the scale of the prints so that there is not too much of any one kind of print.

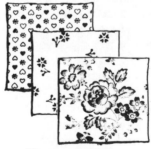

*Choose prints in
several different
scales for texture.*

Today, a very small, regular print in a soft, muted color is often used as the background in place of the more traditional white or off-white solid fabric. Larger, more flamboyant prints such as paisleys, chintzes, or florals are also used, but you'll need to place templates carefully on them. For this reason, it can be very helpful to carry a set of see-thru plastic templates with you while shopping for fabric, so that you can place them in several different positions on the fabric to see what different effects are possible. Spacing templates across the fabric on selected design motifs may also require purchasing extra yardage.

Prints with large designs may look like two different fabrics if you are cutting small patches side by side and the template falls over two different areas of the large design. Therefore, you'll need to plan carefully the placement of templates, or you'll want to choose a print that is fairly uniform in color and detail so that all of the patches appear similar. Widely spaced prints won't work well with small pattern pieces unless they are strategically placed.

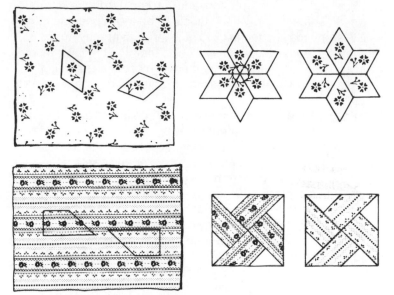

Place templates on parts of a print fabric to get the effect that you desire.

Interesting texture can be added to a quilt design through use of a multicolored print. Accent colors in the print might be repeated in other parts of the quilt. Probably you'll want to use just one of these multicolored prints in order to avoid a busy appearance. Striped fabric can also be used to advantage, especially in sashes and borders. But stripes can overwhelm even while they provide motion and excitement in a design, so use them judiciously. Careful cutting and extra yardage for stripes will probably be necessary.

Type and Quality of Fabric. You will put much time and effort into making your quilt, and you want it to look good for as long as possible. Therefore, be sure to use the best quality fabrics that you can afford. Most quilters seek out medium or dressweight fabrics of 100% cotton as the optimum choice. You should choose fabrics that are firmly woven so that they won't fray or ravel, because the 1/4" seam allowances used in piecing don't allow for much leeway. Loosely woven fabrics may allow quilt batting to seep through to the surface, and they will tend to stretch out of shape, creating unsightly puckers or pleats in the seams. At the same time, you don't want tightly woven fabrics because you will have difficulty quilting through them.

Sometimes a particular color or print or texture is available only in a fabric other than cotton, and you can use these with care. However, some may ravel too much, or be too slippery to handle easily; some may be too thick to quilt through or may not be washable. Choose these for wall quilts that don't receive much wear and tear, or, better yet, try them in more advanced quilt projects after you learn the basics with cotton fabrics that are easy to handle.

Fabric Preparation. Once you have collected all of the fabrics for your quilt, you should prepare them for cutting out patches. Before washing and drying them, test each for colorfastness by immersing them one at a time in warm water and gently squeezing several times. If the water remains clear, proceed to the next fabric. If the water discolors, squeeze, rinse, and refill the sink until the color doesn't run. Discard any fabrics that continue to bleed color, since they'll be a problem in any quilt you make. After all fabrics have been tested, wash them with gentle detergent and a gentle cycle (warm water, cool rinse) in the washing machine. If the various pieces are squarish, you can wash about 10 yards at a time. Only five or six yards will wash well if the pieces are long and narrow such as 1/8- or 1/4-yard lengths or 3 or 4 yard lengths. In order to wash longer lengths of fabric, you should unfold the lengthwise fold, and refold it crosswise before putting it into the machine to avoid wrapping it tightly around the agitator. After washing, dry the fabric at medium heat. If any of it comes out of the dryer heavily wrinkled, and you cannot iron it smooth, discard it because it won't look right next to other, less wrinkly fabrics in the finished quilt. When you are ready to cut out the patches, trim off selvedges and iron the fabric to remove all wrinkles.

Lesson No. 6: Choosing Fillers and Linings

In addition to the fabrics for your first quilt top, you'll need a filler such as a quilt batt or lightweight blanket, some fabric for the quilt lining, thread, and a few other sewing supplies. In this and the following lesson, we'll look at some considerations when selecting each of them.

Cotton Batting. The way you want the finished quilt to look will determine the best kind of filler to put between the quilt top and the lining. In the past, most quilts were filled with a cotton batting, which shifted and became lumpy when the finished quilt was washed unless it had been quilted every 1" to 2" across the quilt. Cotton batting is very soft and allows you to make very small stitches, but it is also rather thin so that the quilt will look somewhat flat when finished. To use a cotton batting, select a glazed-finish batt, and handle it gently when spreading it out to make the quilt "sandwich" (top, batting, and lining). Or, consider a blended cotton batt that has 20% polyester in it to make it more sturdy. This kind of batting may shrink in the finished quilt, so many quilters recommend soaking it in hot water in the washing machine with no agitation, spinning it to remove water, and drying it on the gentle cycle. (This is *not* recommended for a plain cotton batting.) In either case, you'll need to plan on fairly extensive quilting to hold the batt in place.

Polyester Batting. Several kinds of polyester batts are available, and they make a much puffier quilt than does a cotton batt. You should choose a needlepunch or bonded polyester batt because the unbonded ones may become lumpy like cotton batting, and synthetic fibers may migrate through the quilt top to create a "beard" or lint on the quilt surface. Polyester batts are available in ¼" to 1" thicknesses. Choose a thicker batt when you plan to tie the quilt, but not when you want to make small quilting stitches. Polyester batting is lightweight and doesn't wad or get lumpy (unless it is unbonded), so quilting lines may be as far apart as 6" to 8", although most quilters prefer to do more quilting than this. It is helpful to take polyester batts out of the package and unfold them the day before they will be used so that the fibers can relax and fold lines disappear.

Wool and Silk Batting. Wool batting requires close quilting, but it is springy like polyester batting and very warm. Silk batting is most often used for quilted clothing, since it is not available in a large size for quilts, but rather in "leaves" which must be unfolded and layered together to form a batt. It is luxurious and quilts beautifully, but it is expensive and very fragile.

Blankets. Flannel sheet blankets as well as thin woolen or cotton blankets may be used as quilt fillers if they have been well laundered to eliminate shrinkage. The quilting design will not stand out in relief since the finished quilt will be rather flat, but this is a good way to use materials on hand rather than making new purchases. Thicker blankets can be used in a tied quilt, but are probably not a good idea for one that is to be quilted.

Size of Batting. Whatever filler you choose, it should be about 2″ larger on all sides than the quilt top because it will pull in a bit when quilted. Although batting can be spliced to form a larger piece, you'll probably find it is better to use a batt that is already in one piece for your first quilting project. There are many sizes on the market from small (45″ x 60″) for crib-size quilts to very large (120″ x 120″) for king-size quilts, or you can purchase batting by the yard.

Lining Fabric. The fabric you use for the quilt lining should be similar to the fabrics used in the quilt top. Most quilters choose a soft, firmly woven cotton fabric that is easily quilted. Beware of using a bedsheet for the quilt lining. Even though it will eliminate the need for seams on the lining, the very tightly-woven percale fabric is difficult to quilt.

Your quilting stitches and the overall quilting design will show up much better on a lining made of solid-colored fabric. You might wish to choose a print fabric to hide uneven stitches, or when you plan to use several different colors of quilting thread. If you use a print, choose one that won't show through to the front of the quilt. It may be wise to avoid dark colors for the lining since they sometimes show through to the front, giving a darkened cast to the finished quilt.

Size of Lining. Just like the batting, the quilt lining should be cut 2″ larger than the quilt top on all sides. You are likely to need at least one seam to make the lining big enough. Most competition judges prefer vertical seams, although seams may run either vertically or horizontally to make the most efficient use of fabric. If more than one seam is required, try to balance the location of the panels so that seams are symmetrical. The illustrations on the next page suggest some of the possibilities.

Preparing the Lining. To prepare lining fabric, unfold the lengthwise fold and refold crosswise when you put it in the washing machine. Wash and dry it as you plan to treat it after the quilt is finished. Remove all selvedges and press it well before seaming. A machine-stitched seam will be much stronger and more efficient than hand sewing. Sew a ¼″ to ½″ seam, and press the seam open if you are worried about the number of layers of fabric through which you'll have to quilt. A better idea is to press the seam allowances to one side so that batting cannot seep through the seam.

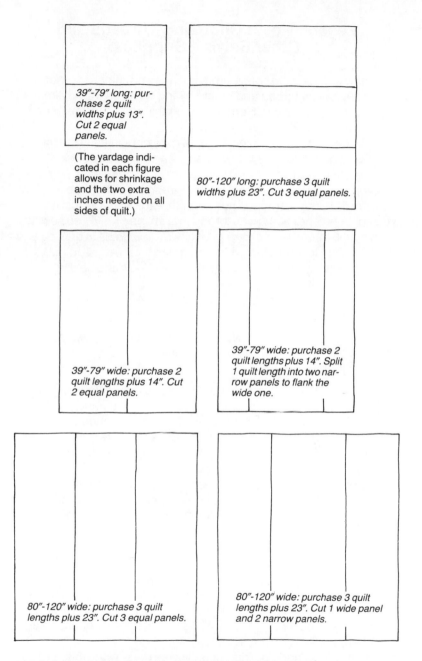

39"-79" long: purchase 2 quilt widths plus 13". Cut 2 equal panels.

(The yardage indicated in each figure allows for shrinkage and the two extra inches needed on all sides of quilt.)

80"-120" long: purchase 3 quilt widths plus 23". Cut 3 equal panels.

39"-79" wide: purchase 2 quilt lengths plus 14". Cut 2 equal panels.

39"-79" wide: purchase 2 quilt lengths plus 14". Split 1 quilt length into two narrow panels to flank the wide one.

80"-120" wide: purchase 3 quilt lengths plus 23". Cut 3 equal panels.

80"-120" wide: purchase 3 quilt lengths plus 23". Cut 1 wide panel and 2 narrow panels.

Lining may need to be pieced in two or three panels, depending on the size of your quilt. Seams can be vertical or horizontal.

Lesson No. 7: Choosing Threads and Other Sewing Supplies

Now that we have considered battings and linings for your first quilt, let's look at thread and other sewing supplies that will make your quiltmaking easier. Here are some things to consider when selecting each of them.

Thread. Thread for piecing, appliqué, or quilting is cut into lengths of about 20″ to 24″ and used as a single strand. Most quilters choose a cotton thread for piecing and appliqué. Thread made totally of polyester can cut the threads in cotton fabrics, but some of the cotton-wrapped polyester threads will work just fine. If you encounter problems with thread that tangles while you sew, try running the thread over a cake of beeswax (available in quilting and fabric stores) to strengthen and straighten it as well as to make it glide smoothly through the fabric when you do hand sewing.

Run thread over a cake of beeswax to prevent tangles.

Choose thread colors to match the appliqué patches, not the background fabric to which they'll be sewn. When hand piecing, use a color that matches the darker of the two patches. Most machine workers who will be piecing several different fabrics choose a neutral thread color such as beige or gray to avoid constant rethreading of the sewing machine.

Since you will need a lot of basting thread when making a quilt, choose any inexpensive, light-colored thread. (A darker color may leave marks on the fabric.) Many quilters find that a light color other than the one they are using to do the appliqué or quilting makes removing the basting thread easier.

Thread for Quilting. When it is time to quilt the three layers (top, batting, and lining) together, many quilters choose the same thread that they would use to do piecing or appliqué work. If the quilt will be washed often or receive hard use, you may wish to choose a quilting thread. This is a somewhat thicker cotton thread, and there are several brands available.

In the past, hand quilting usually was done with white or off-white thread, and the Amish often used black thread. Today there is a wide variety of colors on the market, and you might choose any thread color that complements your work. (Remember that a contrasting color will show off your stitches, so if you are worried about uneven stitches, a matching color will help to make them less obvious.) Some quilters use several different colors on the same quilt, and this might look strange on the back. You may want to use a printed fabric lining or plan to hang such a quilt so that the back won't be seen.

Needles. Piecing and appliqué work can be done with needles called "sharps," which are long and thin—probably the same kind that you already have in your sewing basket. Many quilters prefer to use the same needles that are used for quilting. These are called "betweens" or, sometimes, "quilting" needles. The higher the size of the needle, the smaller it will be, and smaller needles will allow you to do smaller stitches. A beginning quilter should start with a #8 between. But you'll want to buy a package of assorted sizes and experiment to see which number works best for you. Most quilters are soon using a #9 or #10 needle, and some find a #11 or #12 is

#5 sharp

#5 between

#9 sharp

#9 between

Needles: most quilters use sharps or betweens for piecing and betweens for quilting. The bigger the number, the smaller the needle.

best. Whenever a needle becomes sticky or burred, discard it immediately and treat yourself to a brand new one. They're inexpensive, and one that glides smoothly through your quilt fabric is indispensable.

Thimbles. There are many kinds of thimbles on the market, and this sewing tool is absolutely necessary for saving your fingers and helping you to push the needle through several layers of fabric and batting. It may feel awkward at first, but learn to use one, and you'll never stop quilting!

Thimbles are usually worn on the middle finger of the sewing hand while piecing, appliquéing, or quilting. You are likely to purchase a metal thimble, and it should fit snugly, but not so tightly that it hurts. (There are also leather thimbles on the market, and if you choose one of these, pick a very snug one since they will tend to stretch with use.) You may also find that you need a "winter" and a "summer" thimble because changes in the ambient temperature may cause changes in the size and shape of your finger. Your thimble should not be rounded or smooth on top. It should have grooves or ridges to catch the blunt end of the needle and help you guide it through the layers of fabric. These grooves or ridges may be on the end of the thimble or on the sides, depending on how you personally like to sew. Purchase an inexpensive thimble or borrow one to see what works best for your sewing style.

Thimbles come in various styles and materials. Experiment to see what works best for you.

When they are quilting, some quilters also wear a thimble on the index finger of the hand below the quilt sandwich to protect that finger from the prick of a needle. Others cover their index finger with clear nail polish, or work on building up a good callous. You'll want to try out several methods to see which works best for you.

Pins. You'll need a package (100 or more) of fine dressmakers' pins to use while appliquéing or piecing. These pins should be narrow and smooth so that they make small holes in the fabric and slide through it easily. You'll want pins with sharp points, not ball-point pins. Discard any with burrs immediately. The pins should be rustproof also, and it is wise to leave them pinned to the fabric only as long as necessary to finish each activity, so that they never have a chance to leave permanent marks. Colored glass heads on pins give you good visibility and handling ease, but the larger heads are not good for machine piecing since they don't lie flat in the fabric.

Scissors. You'll also want to have at least three different kinds of scissors in your quilting basket. One pair will be needed for cutting out paper, cardboard, or plastic templates. Another pair should be kept exclusively for cutting fabric, and they should easily and accurately cut through several layers. You'll also need to have a pair of sharp embroidery scissors for small-scale cutting chores such as trimming threads or clipping into seam allowances.

Your quilting basket will need three kinds of scissors: paper scissors, embroidery scissors, and fabric scissors.

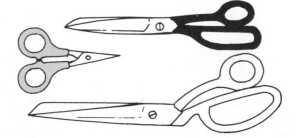

Lesson No. 8: How to Make Templates for Piecing and Appliqué

One of the most important steps in sewing accurate patchwork takes place before you pick up needle and thread. First you need to make accurate templates with which to mark the fabric for cutting patches.

Types of Templates. Most quiltmakers use templates that are the exact size of the finished pattern. When they mark the fabric, they place the template so that an extra ¼" of fabric is left outside of each marked line for a seam allowance for hand piecing, or ³⁄₁₆" turn-under allowance for hand appliqué. If the quiltmaker plans to do machine piecing, the templates should include the ¼" seam allowance in the template. To do this, accurately trace each pattern piece; then use a ruler to mark additional ¼" lines *outside* of all sides of each template. Cut on the outer lines, and use these larger-sized templates to mark and cut the fabric. (Line up the template right beside the previously marked patch without extra space for seam allowances between patches because the seam allowance is already included in the template.) Some quiltmakers prefer to make window templates, that is, templates open in the middle to allow for both a seam line and a cutting line. As a beginning quilter, you may find it advantageous to have both lines marked on the fabric to guide you when cutting *and* sewing. However, depending on the technique you use (hand or machine work), you will just need one or the other marked line later on.

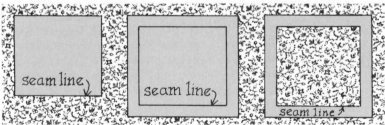

Template without turn-under or seam allowances for appliqué or hand piecing.

Template with seam allowance added for machine piecing.

Window template for hand or machine piecing.

Materials. Templates may be made from heavy paper (such as an index card), lightweight cardboard, tagboard, or a lightweight plastic. The template material needs to meet three criteria to be completely satisfactory. First, the material should be readily available and inexpensive; it should be easy to mark and easy to cut to accurate dimensions; and, finally, it should be durable enough to last to the end of the project. Paper patterns work well for ten or fewer markings; cardboard or tagboard will last for about 40 markings; and plastic templates usually last forever.

Making the Template. You may need tracing paper to help transfer the design to paper, cardboard, or opaque plastic (such as a coffee-can lid). Trace the pattern piece accurately with a fine-point pen or pencil and use a ruler to keep lines straight and corners square. Glue the tracing to the template material; then cut out the pattern shape very carefully—right on the marked line, not beside it. Verify the template size and shape by placing it over the original full-size pattern piece. If you've made any errors—even tiny ones—now is the time to make the template over again. If you mark around an inaccurate template and cut out 200 fabric patches, you will compound your single error 200 times! Another good idea is to test your templates by making one sample block *before* cutting out the rest of the patches.

See-thru Templates. There are several advantages to using "see-thru" template plastic, which is available in art-supply or craft stores and from many mail-order quilt suppliers. Not only does the plastic make a durable template that can be used for many repeated markings, but also you can trace a pattern piece directly onto the plastic without using tracing paper as a middle step. Another advantage of the see-thru plastic is that you can place the template on the fabric and see where to center a particular motif or line up the template in a certain way to add something special to your quilt design. You may wish to mark two perpendicular lines across the center of the templates to make positioning them on the fabric more precise.

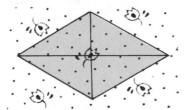

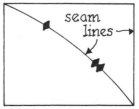

Center of template marked to aid in positioning template on fabric.

Mark notches on seam line of pattern piece for curved seams.

Curved Seams. If you are making templates with curved lines that interlock, add a small notch at the curve *on the seam line* of both pattern pieces. If you also mark these notches in the seam allowance of the fabric patches, there will be a matching set of notches through which you can pin to match seam lines of the curved pieces before seaming them together. Some longer curves may require two or three matching notches.

Labeling and Storing. Once you are sure that you have accurate templates, you should label each one with the quilt name and the pattern-piece number or letter. Be sure to mark those templates that require both sides of the template to be used—in other words, a pattern piece and its reverse. (Many quiltmakers indicate this to themselves by adding the letter "r" to the pattern number or letter; example: "A and Ar" means pieces A and A reversed.) If there is enough room on the template, you may also wish to include the number of patches to be cut from it. Another good idea is to mark the grain line with an arrow. (See pages 33, 36, and 52 for more about grain lines.) Because the template material may be slippery when laid on fabric, some quiltmakers glue a small piece of fine sandpaper to the underside of their templates.

Store the templates together in an envelope so that they won't get separated from each other or lost. You might wish to mark the envelope with the name of the quilt, its finished dimensions and block size, a lettered sketch of the block, and the year in which you are making it.

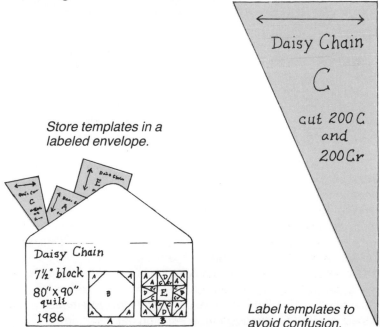

Store templates in a labeled envelope.

Daisy Chain

C

cut 200 C
and
200 Cr

Label templates to avoid confusion.

Daisy Chain
7½" block
80" x 90" quilt
1986

Lesson No. 9: How to Mark and Cut for Hand or Machine Piecing

As we discussed in the previous lesson, accurate templates are the first step toward perfect patchwork. The second and third steps are accurate marking and accurate cutting of the fabric. Here are some hints on how to accomplish these two steps so that the next one—sewing the patchwork—will be accurate later on.

Sample Block. After fabric has been washed to preshrink it and remove excess dye, you should cut off the selvedges and press fabric smooth with an iron. Before marking and cutting all of the quilt pieces, cut out one sample block and piece it together to see if everything fits.

Marking Patches. Mark all pieces on the wrong side of the fabric (usually lighter in color or a bit washed out in appearance) with templates placed *face down*. Mark the border pieces first. There won't be any templates for these, so you should mark them with pencil and yardstick directly onto the fabric along one lengthwise edge. Measure carefully, and remember to add ¼" seam allowances on all four sides of each border piece. It may be wise to add about 2" to 3" extra to the length of each border piece as "insurance"—just in case something doesn't come out as you had planned it, or in case you change your mind later during the construction process and want different border lengths.

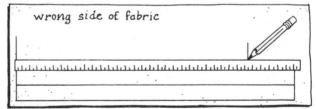

Mark border pieces directly on fabric with pencil and yardstick.

After borders have been marked, measure and mark any triangles for diagonally-set quilts (see page 53), sashes (page 54), or other large pieces before marking the small ones. For hand piecing, the *seam line* is marked, and the templates are placed about ½" apart so that you can cut half way between the two marked lines for a ¼" seam allowance around each patch. If you don't judge distances well, leave more than ½" between patches, since this can be trimmed away after the hand piecing is finished. For machine work, only the *cutting line* is marked with no space required between patches. The accurate cut edge is used to measure the distance from the needle when sewing on the machine.

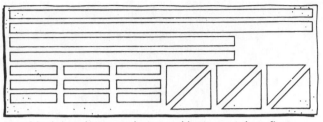

Mark borders, sashes, and large patches first.

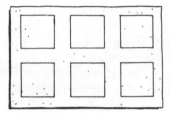

Marking patches for hand piecing: when marking seam line on fabric, leave room between patches to add seam allowance by eye when cutting.

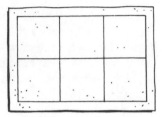

Marking patches for machine piecing: when marking cutting line on fabric, no space between patches is necessary.

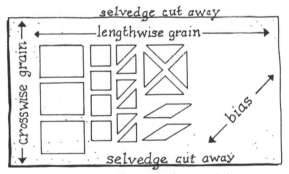

Align templates so that straight grain of fabric will be on outside edges of block.

Grain Line. When placing the templates on the fabric, consider the grain line. It is best to have a straight grain along the outside edges of each block, so study your block drawing and notice which patches touch the outside edge. Place the pattern templates on the fabric so that this same edge lies along the straight grain (either lengthwise or crosswise). It is also wise to place as many straight edges as you can along a straight grain, and whenever possible you will want to avoid sewing two bias edges together. The layout shown in the illustration on page 33 suggests a good alignment for several pattern shapes.

Marking Implements. When using templates while marking the fabric, start in one corner and mark a whole row of patches across the crosswise end of the fabric before proceeding to the next row. Use a sharp lead pencil (many quilters use a #2 pencil; others mark with a mechanical pencil) to mark lightly on the fabric. If the fabric is a dark color, use a dressmaker's pencil (available in light blue, pink, or white) and be sure that it stays very sharp. Keep a small hand-held pencil sharpener in your quilting basket for this purpose, because an accurate, thin marked line is very important. Be especially careful about marking exact corners—the straight lines can be sewn easily even if some of the marking is very light, but you must know where these lines start and stop in order to do precision patchwork.

Cutting Patches. When all of the patches for one fabric have been marked, cut them out with sharp dressmaker's shears—shears that are never used for any other purpose than to cut fabric. For patches that will be hand pieced, you should cut down the center between two marked lines so that approximately ¼" of fabric remains outside each marked seam line of the patch. For patches that will be machine sewn, cut very precisely on the marked cutting lines because these will be the guidelines for sewing on the machine. As a beginning quilter, you will be cutting each patch one at a time. After you gain confidence and experience, you'll find that you can mark one fabric, stack two or three beneath it, and cut several patches at once for machine piecing.

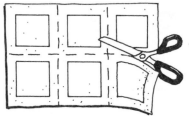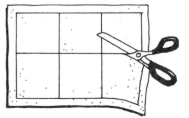

Cutting patches for hand piecing: cut ¼" outward from marked line.

Cutting patches for machine piecing: cut precisely on marked line.

Accuracy. Perfect piecing can be done by either hand or machine. But to make it possible, the patches that you work with must be exactly the right size. Accuracy in making templates, marking, and cutting will all help to make your work look great.

Lesson No. 10: How to Mark and Cut for Hand or Machine Appliqué

Materials. Medium-weight 100% cottons work best for appliqué work because they can be turned under around the edges in a crisp fold. You should wash the fabric to preshrink it and remove excess dye. Trim away both selvedges and press the fabric smooth with an iron.

Sample Block. Before marking and cutting out patches for the entire quilt, cut out all of the pieces for one block and do the appliqué work. (Since appliqué work may draw the fabric in a bit so that the block size shrinks, many quilters add a ½" seam allowance to each background square. After the appliqué work is finished, the block is remeasured and trimmed so that it has the more usual ¼" seam allowance necessary for piecing the blocks together.) Turn under and baste the edges of the individual appliqué patches if doing hand appliqué (no turn-under allowance necessary for machine appliqué), and position all patches on the background block to see if the colors please you and if the shapes fit properly. If there are any problems, make the changes now before cutting out the rest of the quilt.

Marking. First, mark all borders, then sashes (if any), and finally background squares on the *wrong side* of the fabric, just as you would when marking for hand or machine piecing (see pages 32-34). After the borders and sashes, mark the background squares for the quilt blocks. Many quilters find it useful to make a full-size template for these background squares, especially if there are many to be marked. But it is also quite simple to use a pencil and yardstick to mark them. Consider using a drafting triangle with a 90° angle (available in art-supply stores) to ensure that all corners are sharp right angles.

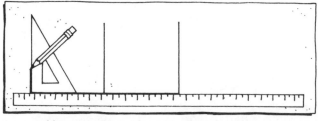

Use a drafting triangle when marking on fabric to insure accurate 90° corners.

Appliqué pieces are usually marked on the *right side* of the fabric so that you can see the turn-under line easily. The marker that you plan to use (whether a #2 pencil, a dressmaker's pencil, or something else) should not run or show through light-colored fabrics. If in doubt, test the marker on a scrap of each fabric you will use—get them wet and use an iron to press them, too, to see if there are any problems—before proceeding.

Spacing Patches. Pattern templates for appliqué are the exact size of the finished patch with no turn-under allowance added. For hand appliqué, mark around the template on the right side of the fabric, leaving enough space between patches to add about ³⁄₁₆″ turn-under allowance on all sides when you cut out the patches. For machine appliqué, the patches may be marked with sides touching, since there is no need for the extra turn-under allowance.

Grain Line. There is no particular grain line rule for placement of appliqué pieces, though you'll find a straight grain is somewhat harder to turn under than a bias one. So it's useful to place templates with their longest part along the bias (or diagonal grain) of the fabric. Using see-through plastic templates will allow you to carefully place them on certain prints or stripes for special effects in the finished work.

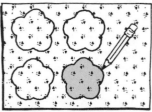

Marking patches for hand appliqué: leave room to add ³⁄₁₆″ turn-under allowance when cutting.

Marking patches for machine appliqué: no turn-under allowance is needed.

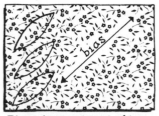

Place longest part of template on bias of fabric.

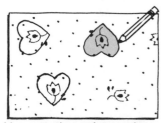

Use see-through templates to position patches on fabric for special effects.

Embroidery. If you plan to do hand embroidery work on the appliqué pieces, you'll find it is a good idea to do the embroidery before cutting out the patches. This will avoid the extra handling that might create frayed edges on small patches.

Cutting Patches. Use very sharp dressmaker's shears when cutting out patches for appliqué. Remember to leave a ³⁄₁₆″ turn-under allowance around all patches that will be hand appliquéd, but cut right on the marked line for machine appliqué.

Stems and Vines. Straight stems should be cut on the straight grain of the fabric. There are two ways to cut out curving stems and vines. You can make a template exactly like the design; then mark and cut as described above. This method does not make very economical use of the fabric, and works best when you need just a few. A second method is to cut bias strips, which are two times the finished width of the stem plus ¼″ for seam allowances. (A ⅛″ seam will be sewn as described on page 44.)

Cut bias stripping for appliquéd stems.

Lesson No. 11: How to Hand Piece

Piecing a quilt by hand is a soothing and relaxing pastime. You can sew a couple of patches together while watching TV, sitting in a doctor's reception area, or waiting to pick up your children after school. Here are some pointers to get you started.

Sewing Order. The first thing you'll need to do is to decide the order in which you will put the patches together. Lay out all of the patches for one block on a table or tray and look for smaller sections or units that you can sew together first, such as two triangles seamed together to form a square, or two squares sewn side by side to form a row. Once the smaller units have been sewn, look for ways to sew units together in larger units or rows. Then sew larger units or rows together to form the block. Whenever possible you should work toward longer and longer straight seams, but not seams that require turning a corner. Some quilt blocks will be started at the center, and single patches or units of patches will be added around the edges. Again, try to avoid making seams that must turn corners.

THIS   NOT THIS

Combining units in straight seams is easier than turning a corner.

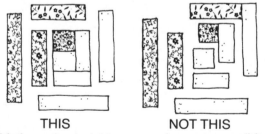

THIS   NOT THIS

Add pieces in straight seams whenever possible.

Pinning. When you are ready to hand sew two patches together, place them right sides together, and put a pin through the end of one marked seam line. Turn the patches over, and be sure that the pin came out exactly at the end of the seam line on the other side. Leave the pin loose (not brought back through to the first side) while you put a pin through the other end of the seam line and check the second side to see that the pin came through at the exact end of that seam line. If the seam line is more than two inches long, or if it is on the bias, you'll probably want to add a pin or two along the seam line, again checking to be sure that it comes out exactly on the seam line on the other side. When both seam lines are aligned, you may wish to bring the pins back to the first side to secure, though not all experienced quiltmakers feel it is necessary.

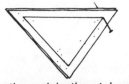

Pin through both patches at the exact end of the seam line.

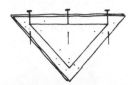

Secure pins when seam lines are precisely aligned.

Thread. Use a single strand of thread about 20″ to 24″ long in a color that either matches or blends with the two patches to be sewn together. Usually it is best to match the darker of the two fabrics, or the solid-colored fabric if one is a print and one a solid, or a color that both prints have in common when using two prints. All-cotton or cotton-wrapped polyester thread is less likely to tangle than other threads. Put a single knot in one end with a fairly long tail (about 1″).

Piecing. When hand piecing two patches together, you sew from seam line to seam line, not from edge to edge. Make a running stitch with about 8 to 10 stitches per inch. Begin at one end of the seam line by removing the pin and making a single stitch. Pull the thread all of the way through, hold the thread tail out of the way, and repeat the stitch twice in the same place making two backstitches. Bring the loose tail down along the seam line and hold in place while you proceed forward along the seam line with a running stitch that catches the tail. Remove pins as you sew, and check the other side frequently to be sure that your stitches are exactly on that seam line, too. When you reach the other end of the seam, take two

Start each seam with a single stitch.

Secure beginning of seam with two backstitches.

backstitches that come out right at the corner, and then weave the thread back through three or four of the running stitches just made. Clip this thread, and also trim anything left of the thread tail at the beginning of the seam.

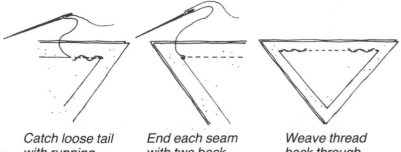

Catch loose tail with running stitch as you sew the seam.

End each seam with two back-stitches.

Weave thread back through running stitches and clip.

Look carefully at the finished seam on both sides to be sure that the stitching follows the marked seam line and that there are no puckers or gathers in the seam. Correct any errors now.

Although most quilters do not thoroughly press hand-pieced quilt blocks until all of the seams are finished, you may wish to finger press (firmly crease between the fingers, not with an iron) the finished seam to one side, usually toward the darker fabric. When joining longer seams that have other seams at right angles to them, sew them without stitching down the seam allowances, making a tiny backstitch immediately before the loose seam allowances, passing the needle through the allowances, and making another tiny backstitch immediately after the allowances before continuing to the other end of the seam.

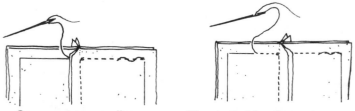

Sew past seam allowances without stitching them down.

Lesson No. 12: How to Machine Piece

Machine piecing is efficient, and you can easily learn how to do it. With a little practice, you'll find that you can make a whole quilt top very quickly and that the seams in it are quite strong. Multiple mistakes can be made quickly, too, so it is wise to plan ahead with this method.

Sewing Order. You will need to decide the order in which the patches will be sewn together. (Review the discussion about this on page 38). You will find it very helpful to machine piece one complete block to check this joining order as well as to decide to which side a seam allowance will be pressed before the next seam is sewn. Hang this block above your sewing machine for a quick reference while you make the rest of the quilt blocks.

Machine piecing is generally done from edge to edge rather than from seam line to seam line. Since these patches are cut with an exact ¼" seam allowance on all sides and have no marked seam line, you will need to use the width of the machine presser foot or a mark on the machine's throat plate to guide you. Carefully measure the distance from the needle to the outer right edge of the presser foot. If the distance is ¼", you will be able to line up the fabric edge with the edge of the presser foot while sewing. If this distance is not ¼", you should carefully measure ¼" to the right of the needle on the throat plate, and place a piece of masking tape there to use as a guide.

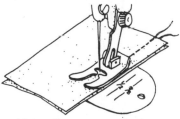

Using the presser foot as a seam gauge.

Using masking tape to mark the ¼" seam allowance.

Seam Allowances. While doing machine piecing, you cannot avoid sewing down the seam allowances that are crossed by the seam you are sewing, so it is important to plan ahead and decide to which side a seam allowance will be pressed—usually toward the darker fabric. If there are two seams to be crossed at the same spot, smooth the seam allowance on the under layer *away* from the needle, and the allowance on the top layer *toward* the needle to ensure a good match and a less bulky seam. Points will have two lines of stitching that form an X on the wrong side of the fabric. Aim the needle at the center of the X when you join the adjacent patch for a perfect point.

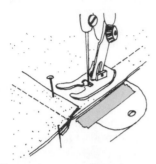

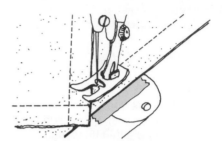

Smooth seam allowances in opposite directions for a less bulky seam.

Aim for the center of the stitched X to assure a perfect point.

Time-Savers. You will save time by piecing assembly-line style. For example, you might sew all of the A triangles to the B triangles before joining the resulting A-B unit to the C squares. You will also save thread and time by "chaining" units together. For example, line up an A triangle with a B triangle (cutting off the corners will make this even easier), and feed them under the needle an exact ¼" from the cutting line. Sew from edge to edge, and stop the machine. Without cutting the thread or lifting the presser foot, align and then seam another A triangle to a B triangle in the same way. There may be a couple of extra stitches between the sewn patches, but do not let the patches overlap. After sewing many patches together in this manner, carefully snip the newly made units apart.

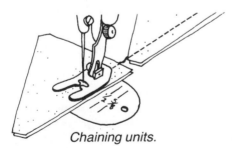

Chaining units.

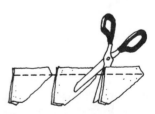

Snipping apart chained units.

Lesson No. 13: How to Hand Appliqué

Here are some pointers to make your appliqué smooth and neat. When appliqué patches are free form, you can pin them to the background fabric and appliqué them by turning under the allowances as you go along. If the arrangement of patches is more precise, you will find it useful to baste under the allowances first so that you can place patches exactly where they need to be in relation to other patches. Then pin or baste them in place on the background fabric before appliquéing.

Basting. To baste, fold the allowance to the wrong side just inside the marked pencil line (so it won't show), and baste in place with running stitches, using a light-colored thread. Do not turn under or baste any edges that will be tucked under other appliqués.

Clipping. When basting convex curves, use a pair of very sharp embroidery scissors to clip into the seam allowance to a depth of about ⅛". Clip along the curve every ¼" or a bit closer so that the fabric allowance will stay smooth underneath. On concave curves you may need to clip almost to the marked seam line.

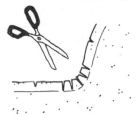

Clip ⅛" into allowances on convex curves.

Clip almost to seam line on concave curves.

On inner points clip almost to the seam line, and when appliquéing, you'll need to put a few extra stitches right at that point to hold it in place. When basting under sharp points, it helps to trim some of the excess fabric at the point. Then turn down the point, turn under one side, and then the other.

Strengthen inner points when appliquéing.

Trim excess fabric from seam allowances when basting under sharp points.

Stems. To prepare narrow stems for appliqué, fold bias strips in half lengthwise with *wrong sides together,* and sew a ⅛″ seam. Fold the two seam allowances under, keeping the stitching just inside the fold line, and press. When appliquéing these curved stems in place, stitch the concave curves (ones that dip inward) first before stitching the outer curves.

Press seam allowance and
seam under bias strip.

Appliqué the inside curve first.

Circles. To make perfect small circles, cut a thin cardboard circle that is the finished size, and cut the fabric circles with a ¼″ seam allowance added. Sew a running stitch within the seam allowance, place the cardboard circle in the center of the wrong side of the fabric, and pull the circle up around the cardboard. Lightly press the fold line in place, and remove the cardboard.

Placement. When you are ready to appliqué, make placement guidelines on the background fabric by folding it in half diagonally, vertically, and horizontally. Draw similar lines on the block drawing (if not already included) to guide you in placing the patches. If you prefer, place the background fabric over the full-sized block pattern and lightly trace the placement lines for main patches. Then pin or baste appliqués in place on the background fabric.

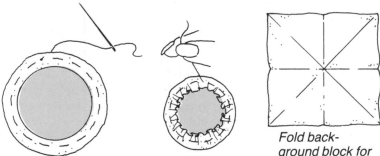

Gather seam allowance around
cardboard for perfect circles.

Fold back-
ground block for
placement
guidelines.

Appliquéing. Stitch the patches in place by working from the background forward. In other words, sew the patches that are in back of other patches first, then add other layers as required. The last patches to be added are the ones on top. The edges of any underlying patches are not usually turned under. It is also helpful to cut away the background fabric from behind appliqués as you work so that there will be fewer layers of fabric to quilt through later.

Use about 20″ to 24″ of a single strand of thread that matches the color of the appliqué patch. The stitch to use is a blind stitch that shows just a tiny spot of thread on the front and a slightly longer (⅛″) length of thread on the back. Bring the thread up through the background fabric and catch just a couple of threads of the fold of the appliqué patch. Push the needle down through the background right above the spot where it came up, and move the needle about ⅛″ away to come up through the background and patch again. Pull stitches firmly but not too tightly. Make all beginning and ending knots or backstitches on the back, and weave loose thread ends into stitches under turn-under allowances on back so that they won't show through background fabric later when quilt top is placed over batting. When appliqué work is finished, remove basting threads carefully, and clip away any excess background fabric from underneath.

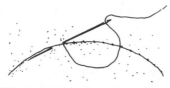

Blind stitch for hand appliqué.

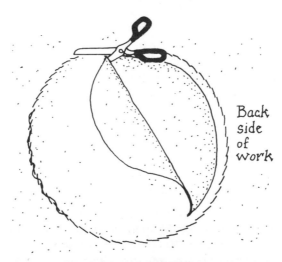

Back side of work

*Cut away background fabric
from behind appliqués.*

Lesson No. 14: How to Machine Appliqué

If you are comfortable working with a zigzag sewing machine, you will find that machine appliqué is a quick and easy way to make sturdy decorations for clothing and quilts. You will be cutting out fabric patches with no seam allowances, basting or gluing them in position on a background fabric, and using a satin stitch (a very close zigzag stitch) to secure the edges of each patch. Here are some ideas to help you get started with the technique.

Fabrics. Machine appliqué allows you to use almost any kind of fabric from sheer voiles or lawns to heavy corduroys or velvets. As a beginning quiltmaker, you will probably have the best success with medium-weight fabrics such as cottons or cotton blends.

Thread. Choose an extra-fine, 100%-cotton, machine-embroidery thread for the top of your machine, and use any good cotton or poly/cotton thread for the bobbin. Machine appliqué is generally done with thread colors that match the appliqué patches, and this is a good idea for beginning projects when you are still refining your technique. However, machine appliqué stitching is more noticeable than hand appliqué stitching, so the machine stitches may be decorative as well as functional. You may wish to consider using a contrasting thread color for special effects, or all black or dark gray thread that creates an outline for each patch.

Preparation and Placement. Some quilters stabilize the fabric by fusing an iron-on interfacing to the back of each patch. Before using the satin stitch to appliqué patches in place, you will need to position them securely on the background fabric. You can use a glue stick or hand basting to hold the patches in place. Then machine sew a basting stitch (about 6 to 8 stitches per inch) or a very open zigzag stitch around the patch about 1/16″ from the edge. This stitching line will anchor the patch in place, and you can make any adjustments necessary if it puckers.

Machine baste the appliqué patches in place.

Satin Stitch. You'll want to do a practice piece with the satin stitch to get the tension right on the sewing machine as well as to choose the stitch width and check the thread color. Use the same number of layers of scraps from the fabrics you'll use in the finished piece. Most machine appliquérs loosen the top tension on the machine just a bit so that the stitches interlock underneath the fabric layers and no bobbin thread shows on the top at all. The main part of the satin stitch should be over the appliqué patch with only a little into the background fabric so that the patch won't fray. The fabrics you choose will determine the width of the satin stitch that you use, as finer fabrics pucker less with a narrow satin stitch, while heavier fabrics may require an extra-wide stitch to keep them from fraying. Most medium-weight cottons will work best with a satin stitch that is about ⅛" wide and close enough to smoothly cover the stitched area without bunching.

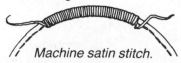

Machine satin stitch.

For the neatest beginning and ending of the satin stitch, leave a long thread tail, which is pulled through to the back of the work and knotted. Thread the loose ends into a sewing needle and weave into the back of the satin stitch for an inch or two; then clip off excess thread.

When you reach a corner with the satin stitch, leave the needle in the background fabric, lift the presser foot, and adjust the angle of the fabric. Then lower the presser foot and continue stitching.

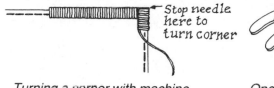

Turning a corner with machine satin stitch.

Open-toed appliqué or buttonhole foot.

Sewing Machine Maintenance. Machine appliqué requires a large amount of stitching, which means that there may be a heavy lint buildup in the machine as well as several dulled needles. In order to do good machine appliqué, you'll need to clean and oil the sewing machine often and replace needles frequently. You probably received a booklet when you purchased your sewing machine that explains the dos and don'ts of zigzag or machine appliqué on your particular machine. Don't forget to refer to it if you have any problems as you work. If you find that you really like this technique, you may wish to purchase the open-toed appliqué or buttonhole foot available for most zigzag machines. The open space between the toes allows you to see the stitching more easily, and a groove on the underside of the foot allows the ridge of satin stitching to move more smoothly under the presser foot.

Lesson No. 15: Blocking and Pressing

When constructing individual quilt blocks, you "finger press" the pieced seams or the appliquéd turn-under allowances—that is, press the fabrics between finger and thumbnail just enough to hold a crease where you want it—rather than using an iron after each seam is completed. As you progress from seam to seam, you should check to see that there are no puckers or gathers and that the stitches are exactly where you want them.

Checking the Blocks. Once all of the blocks are finished, measure all sides of all blocks to be sure that each is finished the same size. If any of the blocks is too large or too small to be joined to the others, now is the time to plan for compensating. It may be possible to have extra wide seam allowances on a too-large block—or narrower than usual allowances on one that's too small—so that the finished dimensions will be the same as on other blocks. (You'll want to mark such blocks with a note to remind you which need special seams.) If this is impossible, take apart some of the seams in a block and improve them so that the block is the same size as the rest of the quilt blocks. *Now* is the time to make changes and corrections before you have put together so much of the quilt top that you will have difficulty fixing blocks that puff out or pull in.

Ironing vs. Pressing. There is a difference between ironing and pressing a quilt block, and the technique that you use can affect the finished quilt top. When ironing, you move the iron across fabric, smoothing wrinkles as you go. Usually you iron something on the right side of the fabric, and it has just a few, fairly long seams with wide seam allowances. Quilt blocks, however, have very short, narrow seams, with allowances pressed to one side of the seam line on the wrong side of the fabric. Press them by lifting the iron and setting it down on each new area of the block without moving the iron across the fabric. On pieced blocks this will prevent distorting the design by pushing a seam line out of shape. When pressing appliqué blocks, you should try to press only the background fabric whenever possible, so that the turn-under allowances under the appliqués do not get crushed against them creating shiny spots on the surface. You should also be careful not to crush any appliqué blocks that have extra padding or embroidery stitches added to them.

Blocking. All of the blocks should be truly square—that is, the four corners should be accurate right (90°) angles. If some of your blocks have gone askew, they should be straightened *now* before becoming a part of the quilt top where they will be forever crooked. To square them up (or "block" them), first draw a true square that is the exact size of the block plus seam allowances on the ironing-board cover. (A needlepoint marker is good for this purpose, but not a water-soluble marking pen which will disappear under steam.) Place a quilt block right side down on the ironing board, and pin it in several places along each edge so that the block fits in the marked square, and all corners are at right angles. Cover the block with a damp cloth and press, or use a steam iron. Gently steam press the edges of the block until straight. Then press the center of the block.

Pressing Seams. Pressing the quilt blocks is an important step, whether they need to be blocked or not, and you'll want to think about your quilting plans while you do this. Try to press seams away from areas where you wish to quilt close to a seam line, or adjust your quilting plans to avoid the seam allowances whenever possible. In pieced blocks, all seams should be pressed to one side—not open—so that there will be a layer of fabric under the seam line to strengthen it, and so that the fabric layers hold the batting inside the quilt. It is wise to press seams toward a darker fabric whenever possible so that dark seam allowances don't show through light-colored fabric. If this is impossible, trim the darker fabric seam allowance slightly narrower than the lighter one. (If you are doing machine piecing, you should trim such seam allowances *before* the fold is sewn down into the next seam.)

There should be as few layers of fabric under any particular spot as possible. If you are pressing a spot where many seams come together, it is best to press all of the seams in the same direction, either clockwise or counterclockwise, so that all of the layers of seam allowances create a less bulky "swirl" where they meet. Curved seams can be pressed in either direction, though it may prove helpful to make several short clips into the seam allowance to facilitate making them lie flat.

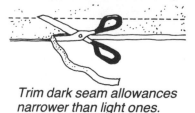

Trim dark seam allowances narrower than light ones.

Press seam allowances into a swirl where several seams meet in one spot.

Ironing Blocks. Once each block has been pressed gently on the wrong side, you can turn it over and *iron* the right side. Iron with the grain whenever possible, and avoid ironing on the bias. Many quiltmakers only *press* their quilt blocks, and wait until the whole quilt top is finished before ironing on the right side.

49

Lesson No. 16: How to Set Blocks Together

Revising Setting Plans. When all of the blocks for your first quilt have been completed and are well blocked and pressed, you will be ready to lay them out on the bed for which they are intended. Even though you may have a prearranged plan (developed in your quilt plan on paper), it is wise to complete all of the blocks before setting the top together so that you have a chance to distribute the blocks uniformly. Now is the time to be sure that the effect is what you had intended. Perhaps you'll decide that alternating the blocks with plain ones would look better, or that sashing would improve the overall appearance. If the blocks do not cover the top of the bed as you had anticipated, perhaps you'll want to make another row of blocks to be added to one side or to the bottom, or maybe you'll need to add sashing. Now is also the time to check your plans for the border: Will it be too narrow? Too wide? Make plans *now* to compensate for anything you forgot to do earlier in your paper plan.

Keeping Track. When the layout of the quilt pleases you, begin to sew the blocks together. The general principle is to sew blocks into rows, and then sew the rows together to finish the quilt top. If you can't leave them out on the bed while doing the sewing, carefully stack blocks from one row together in the order that you plan to sew them, and pin a piece of paper with the row number to the top block. Repeat for all of the rows, and then work with each stack to make the single rows. When a row is finished, leave the piece of paper in place on one of the blocks to remind you of the order in which you'll sew the rows together later on.

Joining Blocks. The seams between blocks or rows are much longer than the ones you made when sewing the patches of a block together, so it is wise to pin them together carefully before sewing, matching seam lines exactly. If any of the seams don't fit properly, take those seams apart *now* and repair them. It's your last chance! Join the blocks together with ¼″ seam allowances. Unless you feel comfortable working at the sewing machine, you may find it is best to do this step by hand so that you can match exactly the seam lines in the blocks and especially the corners of the blocks.

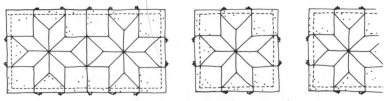

Pin, then sew the blocks together to make a row.

Joining Rows. After the horizontal rows of blocks are completed, you will sew the rows together in long seams until the quilt top is finished. Before sewing, it will be helpful to press all of the seam allowances between blocks in odd-numbered rows in one direction and the seam allowances between blocks in even-numbered rows in the other direction. Then, when rows are sewn together, these seam allowances will be less bulky with fewer layers at one spot.

You'll find it is easiest to sew row 1 to row 2; then sew row 3 to row 4, and so on, through the last pair of rows. Next, sew the seam between rows 2 and 3; then sew the seam between rows 6 and 7 and so on, so that you have groups of four rows together. Finally sew the one or two remaining seams to finish the quilt top.

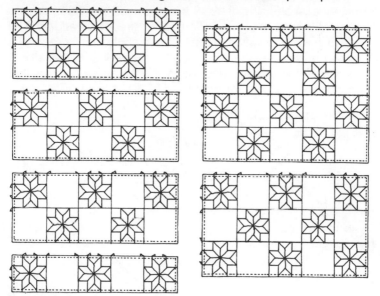

Sew rows 1-2, 3-4, and 5-6. Then sew rows 2-3 and 6-7. Finally, sew seam 4-5 to complete top.

When joining the rows, you should match seam lines exactly. Pin at each seam line, then ease or stretch the fabric to fit. (Slight puckering will be unnoticeable when the top has batting and quilting added, but if there are any large gaps or overlaps, you should adjust them *now.*) When ready, join the rows together with a ¼"-wide seam, just as you did when joining the blocks.

Setting Blocks On the Diagonal. A quilt with diagonally set blocks is just as easy to set together as one with blocks set in horizontal rows. The only difference for a diagonal set is the addition of half-square and quarter-square triangles to fill in the edges of the quilt.

Half and Quarter Squares. You will need four of the quarter-square triangles for the corners of the quilt, and enough half-square triangles to fill in the remaining triangular spaces around the edge, depending on the number of blocks used in the quilt. (This is when a quilt plan on paper is especially important so that you can determine how many half-square triangles are needed.)

Grain Line. If the outer edges of a quilt top are on the bias, they can be easily stretched out of shape when binding or finishing the quilt. Therefore, it is a good idea to have all outside edges of the quilt top on the straight (either lengthwise or crosswise) grain of the fabric. At least one side of every triangle used in a diagonally set quilt top will have a bias edge. Plan so that these bias edges will be added to the quilt top with the side of the triangle that has a straight edge on the outside edge of the quilt. This will insure that all bias sides of triangles will be stabilized *inside* the quilt top where they cannot be stretched out of shape.

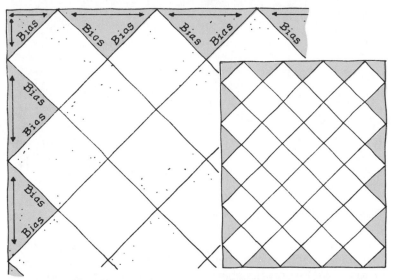

Detail of corner showing bias edges.

Diagonal set with half- and quarter-blocks in gray.

Quarter-square triangles are used on the four corners of the quilt. Therefore, they will need to have two edges on the straight grain of the fabric. A triangular template may be placed on the fabric as shown below. Trace around the template. (Be sure to add ¼" seam allowances on all sides.) You will need only four of these corner triangles for a quilt top.

The half-square triangles will be along the sides of the quilt, with the longest side on the outer edge of the quilt top. Therefore, this longest side of the triangle is the one that should be placed on the grain line (either lengthwise or crosswise) of the fabric. (Remember to add ¼" seam allowances.)

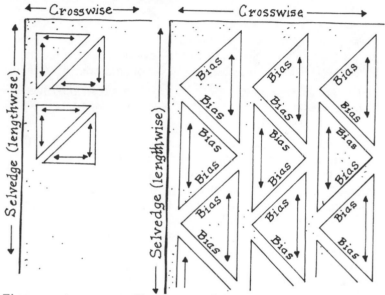

Place quarter-squares like this so straight grain will be on short sides.

Half-square triangles need straight grain on long side.

Joining Blocks into Rows. The blocks are sewn in diagonal rows, beginning with a single block plus two half-square triangles in one corner. Each succeeding row has two more blocks than the previous row plus the half-square triangle on each end. For a square quilt, the center row of blocks will have a quarter-square triangle at each end of the row rather than a half-square triangle. Each succeeding row after the center one will have two fewer blocks than the previous row, until the final row with one block plus two half-square triangles. (A rectangular quilt will have a quarter-square triangle at one end of the two center rows and a half-square triangle at the other end.)

Joining the Rows. When all rows are completed, set them together one after another, just as you would set together a straight-

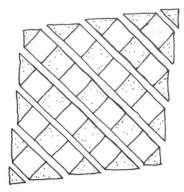

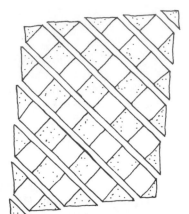

Joining blocks into rows for a square quilt.

Joining blocks into rows for a rectangular quilt.

set quilt top. Then add the last two quarter-square triangles. (You may wish to review the section on joining rows on page 51.)

Setting Blocks with Sashing. Sashing may have many different names—stripping, lattice, cheaters, dividers, rakes—and it has several uses. You can use sashing to make a quilt top bigger, to separate blocks that look too "busy" next to each other, to provide a place for fancy quilting, or as a design element.

Marking and Cutting. Mark and cut sashing on the lengthwise grain of the fabric whenever possible because this grain line is less likely to stretch than the crosswise grain, and the print will more likely be on grain in this direction. Remember to add the ¼" seam allowance on all sides of the sashing pieces and to cut the largest ones first. All of the longer sashes will need markings along their edges where the long sash meets quilt-block or other sashing seams. These may be marked either with a pencil line in the ¼" seam allowance on each side of the sash, or "press-marked" with a warm iron. In the illustration on the next page, a long horizontal sash has been marked to show where quilt-block and sashing seams meet it as well as to show the ¼" seam allowance at each end of the sash. Measure and mark all long sashes in this way.

Marking sashing strip with pencil.

Marking sashing strip with iron.

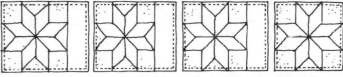

| ¼" | Finished Size of Sashing | | Sashing | | Sashing | | ¼" |

Finished Size of Quilt Block — Quilt Block — Quilt Block — Quilt Block

Long horizontal sash showing block and sashing placement.

Joining Blocks with Sashing. Begin with short sashes and the top row of horizontal blocks. With a ¼" seam, sew a sash to the right-hand side of each of the blocks in the row except the one at the right end. Then join a block/sash to the next block/sash, and continue across the row, ending with the final block that has no sash attached to it. Join the remaining rows of blocks with short sashes in the same way. Press all sashes either toward the sashing (when it is narrow and won't need much quilting) or away from it (when elaborate quilting will be done in the sash).

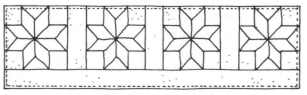

Sew sashing strips to blocks before joining blocks.

Joining Rows with Sashing. Pin a long horizontal sash to the bottom edge of the top row, matching the pencil marks or the ironed creases on the sash with the various seam lines on the block row. Sew the long horizontal sash to the row of blocks with a ¼" seam. Add a long horizontal sash to the bottom edge of each of the other rows of blocks except for the last (bottom) row. Now join the rows of blocks/sashes together as follows: Pin and sew the long sashing strip attached to the bottom of the first row to the top edge of the second row. Continue adding rows of blocks/sashes until the whole top is completed. If the outside row of sashing will have butted seams, add a horizontal sash to the top and the bottom of the quilt. Press all horizontal sashing seam allowances to match the vertical ones (either toward the sashing or toward the block). Add the long vertical sashes to the two side edges of the quilt top. (If mitered corners will be used, add sashes to all four sides leaving

Joining long sashes to block rows.

an extra sashing width free at each corner; then miter using the methods described in the next lesson.)

Setting Squares. To add setting squares to the sashing, sew rows of blocks with short sashing strips not only between the blocks but also on each end of the row. For a sashing row, alternate the setting squares and short sashes, with a setting square on each end. Make enough sashing rows to include one for the top and the bottom of the quilt. Sew sashing rows to the bottom of block rows, sew block/sash rows together, and add a sashing row at the top.

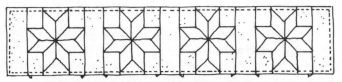

Block/sash row when using setting squares.

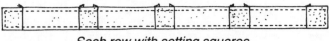

Sash row with setting squares.

Diagonal Sets. To add sashing to a diagonal set, you still follow the same methods as for sashing in a straight-set quilt, but there will be a 45° angle at the ends of each row of sashing. The easiest way to do this is to cut the sashes with 90° angles, and then, after sewing the sashes into the quilt top, trim the excess even with the edge of the quilt top.

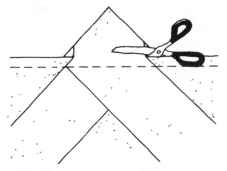

Trim sashing after quilt top is complete for diagonal set with sashing.

Lesson No. 17: How to Miter Borders

To make a quilt lie on a bed or hang on a wall properly without rippled edges or splayed corners, you should measure carefully each step of the way while making the quilt. Templates should be precisely made; fabrics should be marked and cut carefully; and seams should be sewn exactly on the seam line. Once all of the blocks are finished, measure *all* sides of *all* blocks to be sure that they are finished the same size and that all four corners of the blocks are sharp right (90°) angles. Redo blocks that are too crooked or the wrong size.

Measuring the Top. Once the blocks have been set together and gently pressed with an iron, and *before* you add borders to the quilt, it is important to make one final set of measurements. If you have been measuring all along, border strips will be the right size. However, there can be so many variables that it is wise to measure the finished top to see if the border strips need adjustment.

The logical place to measure the finished top is along its outside edges, and this is a useful measurement. You should also measure the width and length of the quilt top across the center. If this measurement is different from that of the outer edges, accidental stretching or inaccurate piecing has occurred, and you will need to ease the outer edges or the border strip to a measurement that equals that of the center of the quilt top.

Mitered vs. Butted Borders. Pieced borders are often designed to fit one full pieced block at each corner of the border with the rest of the side strip filled in with similar pieced blocks. Appliquéd borders or solid strip borders may meet at the corners in either of two ways: side strips may abut end strips at a right angle, or they may be mitered so that the end and side strips meet with a diagonal (mitered) seam.

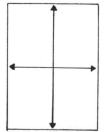

Measure the width and length across the center.

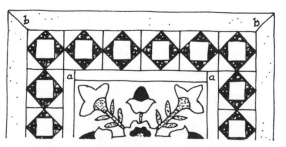

Pieced borders have one full block in each corner; plain borders are either butted (a) or mitered (b).

Length of Border Strips. To measure strips for a border with mitered corners, you will need to know the length of the side to be bordered. Add to this twice the finished width of the border plus ½" for seam allowances. (For example, to add a 2"-wide border to the side of a quilt that measures 63", you will add 63" + 2" + 2" + ½" = 67½" long x 2½" wide strips.) Measure and cut strips for top/bottom and sides of the quilt top to be bordered. (If you plan to cut out the border strips for your quilt before the top is pieced, it is a good idea to add a couple inches extra length for insurance. Once the top is ready for borders, measure the quilt top; mark border lengths with pins; then trim excess *after* mitering.)

Adding the Border to the Top. Once you know what each side measurement should be for the mitered border strip, match and pin the center of the border strip to the center of the side to which it will be sewn, *right sides together.* Also pin at one corner, so that one finished width measurement is extended past the end of the quilt for the miter; then pin the other end. Next, pin the border to the quilt side at each quarter point, then at each eighth point and so on, until pins are about 2" to 3" apart. This will ensure that any necessary easing is done as evenly as possible.

Sew the border strips to the quilt top with a ¼" seam, beginning and ending at the seam line, not at the cut edge of the fabric. If you are sewing the seam by machine, you will have the greatest success if the part to be eased is on the bottom (or away from you), because the feed dogs on the sewing machine have a slight gathering action. If sewing the seam by hand, you may want to have the part to be eased *toward* you so that you can watch for and avoid any tucks or gathers in the seam.

Standard Miter. Mitering the border corners is the final step. A smooth, straight seam at a 45° angle for the miter will ensure a flat corner for the quilt. To make a traditional border miter, place one border over the other at one corner on the wrong side of the quilt. Draw a line from A to B as shown below. Reverse the two borders (bottom one is now on top), and again draw a line from A to B. Match the two pencil lines (fabrics are right sides together), and sew through them. Cut away excess triangular pieces, and press to one side. Repeat this at the other three corners of the mitered border.

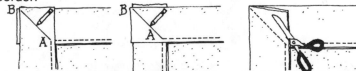

Standard Miter: Mark both border strips, sew along marked lines, and cut away extra triangular pieces.

Easy Ironing-Board Miter. On your ironing board, mark horizontal and vertical lines the same distance apart as the width of the border to be mitered. Draw a diagonal line connecting two opposite corners as shown. Place corner of quilt top wrong side up over guidelines so that border edges fall directly on outside marks. Fold the borders back to the inside so that the two folds are exactly on the diagonal line. Press well. Place a length of *Iron-On Hem Tape* (available at most fabric stores) over folds. Press. (This will hold the miter in position, but allows flexibility for stitching. With right sides together, stitch through the creased diagonal, which is the seam line. Remove tape by pressing again and pulling tape off while still warm. Trim seams just inside the sticky residue left from the tape. Finish other three corners in the same manner.

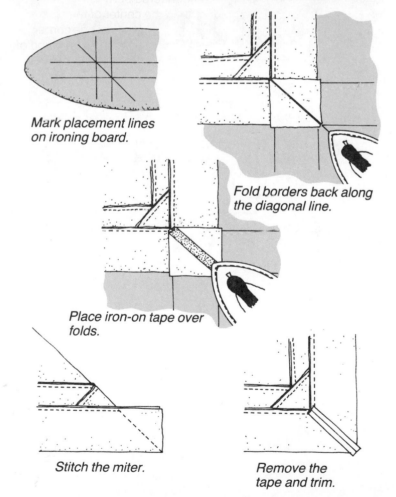

Mark placement lines on ironing board.

Fold borders back along the diagonal line.

Place iron-on tape over folds.

Stitch the miter.

Remove the tape and trim.

Appliqué Stitch Miter. This method for mitering will be easy if you place the quilt top on an ironing board. The borders have been sewn to the quilt top just to the seam line. The top should be right side up with all borders pressed smooth with the iron (not finger pressed). On the lower edge of the quilt top, place the loose horizontal border over the vertical one. At the left corner of the quilt, fold the horizontal border back under itself to form a diagonal fold. Press the diagonal fold and pin in place. Hand stitch the fold with an appliqué stitch. From the back trim away excess fabric.

At the right corner, fold the horizontal border back under itself in the other direction to form the same kind of fold. Press, pin, stitch, and trim as before. Turn the quilt top around, and miter the other two corners in the same manner.

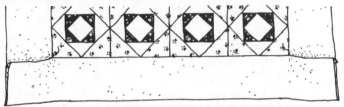

Place loose horizontal border over vertical one.

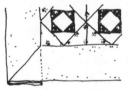

Fold horizontal border under itself along the diagonal.

Hand stitch with appliqué stitch.

Right corner is reversed.

Lesson No. 18: Choosing a Quilting Pattern

A special quilting design will enhance your finished quilt in many ways so it is wise to choose carefully. Many quilt books contain lovely patterns; your local quilt shop sells plastic, cardboard, and paper patterns from many sources; or you can have fun designing your own by using ideas from magazines or books. It will take a little time, but the effort is worth it.

Factors to Consider. Several factors come into play when choosing a quilting pattern. You should consider your skill level as well as the amount of patience and time you are willing and able to commit to the quilting process. The intended use of the quilt is also important: spending a lot of time on an intricate pattern that will receive hard wear and tear on a child's bed, for example, doesn't make sense. However, if you intend to display the quilt on a wall or give it to someone who will appreciate lots of quilting, the extra time and effort put into working an elaborate quilting design will be worthwhile.

The kind of batting that you plan to use may also affect your quilting plans. Polyester bonded batting is usually the best choice for a beginner, and it will retain its shape well. This means that the quilting lines may be as far apart as 6" to 8". Widely spaced quilting may create just the puffy effect that you would like to achieve for a wall quilt, but don't forget that a quilt planned for use on a bed will probably last longer with closer quilting that doesn't put too much stress on each individual stitch.

Quilting Options. The easiest quilting methods are shown on page 64. They are in-the-ditch quilting (a row of stitches along a seam line on the side that has only one layer of fabric) or outline quilting (a row of stitches about ¼" from each seam line). There are several advantages to these methods for the beginning quilter. No quilt marking is necessary, although you may wish to lay down a strip of ¼" masking tape as a guideline for the outline quilting. More often than not, these methods avoid crossing seams where there are extra thicknesses of fabric, and outline quilting also makes the seam allowances underneath less noticeable because the quilting line will be right at the edge of any seam allowances. A viewer's eye will follow a quilting line rather than seeing a slight change in fabric color because of extra layers underneath.

In-the-ditch and outline quilting, however, aren't the only choices. Many of the best contemporary quilts gain visual excitement by contrasting curved quilting lines over the straight seams of a geometric design. On the other hand, a quilt top with curving piecework or rounded appliqués may look terrific with simple straight lines quilted into the background or across the whole design. This means that quilting lines will cross seam lines–and seam allowances where there are two extra layers of fabric–so do this sparingly as a beginning quilter.

Settings that have sashes and setting squares or alternating plain blocks can usually be enhanced with a pretty quilting pattern. To insure that the ¼" seam allowances do not interfere with your quilting plans, you should choose a design that fits inside the space for which it is intended with at least ¼" on all sides between it and the seam lines. If you want to quilt very close to a seam line, you'll need to plan for this during quilt construction and press the seam allowances away from these areas.

Adapting Motifs. Once you find the perfect motif for your quilt design, you may need to adapt it to fit the spaces in which you wish to use it. You can enlarge or reduce the actual design, but more often than not, the printed version you find is really the best size. Enlarging a simple design may leave too many blank, open spaces, or reducing an intricate one may push lines so close together that they can't be quilted effectively. Thus you may find that the best way to use the motif is to rearrange it in its current size to fill the required space.

A large pad of tracing paper will aid you in exploring how to use your design. On one sheet mark off an area representing the actual size of the block patch or sash or border segment you wish to fill. On another sheet trace several repeats of the motifs, cut them apart, and rearrange them to fit the space.

Combining the motif in groups of two, three, or four might fill a space without enlarging the design. Add an extra leaf or a second flower to an existing motif to make it fill the space. Flop or reverse patterns to face each other in pairs or string them together in large or small circles and ovals. Fill the central space in a circular design

Combine quilting motifs with straight-line background quilting to fill a block.

with squares or diamonds, or square up such a circular arrangement by adding straight lines or diamonds outside of the design.

If you really want to use a particular design in a space that is too small for it, try eliminating some lines or a part of the design such as an extra leaf or petal. Single motifs arranged in a row might fill a narrow border or sash. Make them all face the same direction or reverse every other one. Try tilting them to fill borders of different widths, or space them widely with straight or curved lines connecting the motifs.

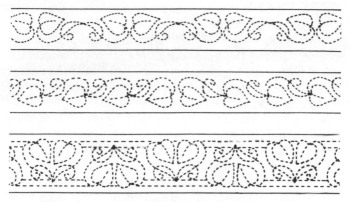

Repeat or reverse quilting motifs to fill a border.

Be sure to look at every design motif with a critical eye. Sketching and resketching until you have a pattern that suits will give you a quilting design that is unique and very personally yours.

Lesson No. 19: Marking a Quilting Pattern

After you've chosen the quilting pattern for your quilt, you must transfer that design to the quilt top. Some quilting lines won't require any marking at all; others can be done with simple techniques that leave no marks behind; and some patterns require more extensive marking, which means that marking tools should be chosen with care to minimize any residue on the quilt. Try all of the following methods to see which one will work best with your quilting plans, and whenever possible choose the method least likely to leave lasting marks on the quilt.

No-Mark Quilting. In-the-ditch quilting (right along the seam line), outline quilting (¼″ from seam lines), and echo quilting (waves of quilted lines rippling outward from appliquéd designs) can be done without marking at all. With a little practice, you can become quite good at quilting parallel lines, judging their distance from the seam line or each other "by eye" and never making any marks on the quilt at all.

Needle Tracking. Another quilting technique that leaves no visible marks on the quilt is needle tracking. Place a template on the fabric surface and lightly scratch around its outline with a needle, or draw freehand with the needle. This line will remain visible long enough for you to quilt along it, although just a short distance or small segment can be done at once since the "markings" disappear quickly as the quilt is handled.

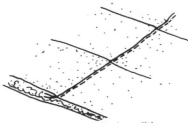

In-the-ditch quilting.

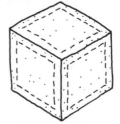

Outline quilting.

Echo quilting.

Needle tracking.

Masking Tape. Straight lines and filler quilting in the background, usually of squares or diamonds, may be marked with a piece of masking tape. Merely position the tape where a line should go, quilt along its edge, and then pull it away. (Caution: Leave the masking tape in place only long enough to quilt along it, but not overnight or for a lengthy period of time, so that any sticky residue will be minimized.) Some simple shapes may be drawn onto self-adhesive CON-TAC® paper, cut out, and peeled from the backing sheet to be used much like masking tape. (There is also a good line of commercial quilting patterns available in peel-away paper.) Again, it is wise to leave the sticky surface attached to the quilt only long enough to quilt around it, and not for a lengthy period of time.

Masking tape.   *Marking around stencil.*

Marking Tools. The cleanest, most washable marker for drawing quilting patterns on a quilt top is a very thin sliver of pure, hard soap. White soaps are especially good for marking dark fabrics, and a colored soap will work on light-colored fabrics, although you should be careful to test the soap on a fabric scrap first to be sure that any dyes in the soap do not remain on the fabric. Any soap residue will wash out of the quilt the first time that it is cleaned if it has not already disappeared when the quilt is handled during quilting and use.

A traditional method for marking a quilt top is to use a well-sharpened pencil. Since this may leave unsightly marks on the quilt that can't be removed, it is wise to use this method with caution. Most quilters suggest a #2 or harder lead pencil because it doesn't leave as much residue and it stays sharpened longer. The pencil line should be very lightly marked, or you can just make a dotted line. If the pencil line is too dark, or if it smudges, remove as much as possible immediately with a white plastic eraser. Usually, any further residue will wash out when laundered after the quilt is finished.

Water-soluble or water-disappearing pens can make marking an intricate quilt design a breeze, but testing them on a scrap of *each* fabric used in the quilt is especially important. Some fabrics may be permanently damaged by the chemicals in water-soluble inks, so it is also important to rinse out all markings very thoroughly with plain water after the quilting is finished. The amount of water needed will depend on how much ink has gone into the fabric, so mark lightly. Wetting the fabric a second time, or soaking it, should remove heavy marks. The markings may turn brownish and become permanent if laundered with soaps or detergents, and they may become permanently imbedded in the fabric if ironed. Be sure to use plain water and don't iron the quilt top before removing the blue markings.

When to Mark. You can trace the quilting design through a single layer of fabric by using a light table or other light source under the design and quilt top. As well, you can draw a line around a stencil, which requires a steady hand and a single layer of fabric. Using either of these methods, you'll want to mark the quilt top before basting together the quilt layers (top, batting, and backing).

Many of these marking methods can be used after the top, batting, and lining have been basted together, and you are ready to quilt. Any method you use to mark your quilt top should be durable enough to last through the quilting step and easily removed once you have finished.

Lesson No. 20: Basting the Quilt Layers

A smooth, beautifully finished quilt with no wrinkles or puckers on the top or lining is what you'll get if you thoroughly baste the quilt "sandwich" before beginning to quilt. It takes a little time and patience, but you'll make up the time because you'll be able to quilt with great confidence and ease. Some quiltmakers use a floor frame or one made from four long boards and C-clamps to do the basting of the quilt layers, and they may not do very extensive basting if the quilt will remain in the frame for the quilting. As a beginning quiltmaker who is more likely to use a hoop than a frame, you'll find that the method outlined below will ensure a well-basted quilt.

Preparing the Top. The quilt "sandwich" includes three layers—the top, the batting or filler, and the lining. The quilt top is the layer that you will have to put the most effort into, and now is the time to be sure that it is perfect on both front and back. Iron it carefully so that you don't stretch any seam lines out of shape and so that you avoid creating tucks or puckers along them. Examine the underside of the quilt top and clip away all threads that might show through the quilt top later on.

Batting. Quilt batting is available in many sizes and you will need a piece that is about 2″ larger on all sides than the quilt top. Reread Lesson No. 6 (page 23) when deciding what kind of batting will work best in your quilt. Open the package and lay the batt on a guest bed overnight before using it so that the folds and rolls of the batt have a chance to relax and lie flat.

Lining. If your quilt is no more than about 40″ on the shorter sides, you will need just one length of lining fabric, but it is more likely that you'll need to make one or more seams on the back side of the quilt. The diagrams on page 25 show the preferred placement for these seams, and on page 24 you will find a discussion about the best fabrics to use. The lining should be about 2″ larger on all sides than the quilt top. Be sure to remove all selvedges before seaming, and press the ¼″ seam allowance to one side so that fibers in the quilt batting cannot seep out through the seam.

Making the "Sandwich." Once all of the wrinkles have been ironed out of the lining, place it wrong side up on a flat surface. Some quiltmakers use masking tape to stretch the lining smooth on a clean floor. Others use a bed or large table and check to see that the lining is straight and wrinkle free.

Spread the batting over the lining, making sure that both pieces are smooth and wrinkle free. Since they will be approximately the same size, their edges should lie one over top of the other. Center the quilt top right side up on the batting so about 2" of batting can be seen on all sides.

Basting. Use a single strand of light-colored thread and a long needle for basting. Make stitches about 1½" to 2" long on the surface and ½" to 1" on the underside. Avoid making a stitch go up or down at exactly the spot where you know quilting stitches will be placed later. Begin basting along one side about ½" from the edge of the quilt top. Make another parallel line of basting stitches about 4" to 6" away from the first one, and continue making parallel lines of basting until you reach the opposite edge of the quilt. As you move toward the center and find it harder to reach the line of basting stitches, roll the already basted portion of the quilt toward the center.

Roll the basted portion of the quilt toward the center as it becomes difficult to reach the spot that needs basting.

When you have reached the other side and basted a last row of stitches about ½" from that edge, smooth the quilt sandwich out again on the flat surface. Move to one of the other sides, and begin basting again in lines that are perpendicular to the first basting rows. Once you are finished, there will be a grid of basting stitches that are no farther than 6" apart. This will insure that the three quilt layers will not shift or pucker when you begin to quilt.

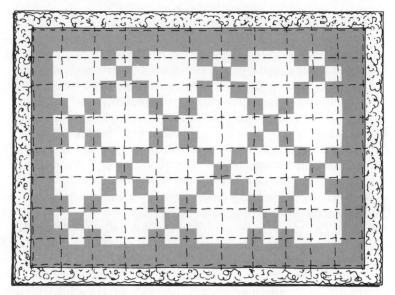

When the basting is complete, you will have a grid of basting lines covering the entire top.

If you will be quilting in a hoop, your work will remain cleaner and neater if you roll the extra two inches of batting and lining to the front of your work and baste them to the edges of the quilt top. Enclosing the batting around the edges prevents batting lint from collecting on the quilt surface, and there will be no loose batting to become tangled and matted while you quilt.

Roll and baste the outside edges of the batting and lining to the front to prevent tangling and matting.

Lesson No. 21: Using a Hoop or a Frame

Hoops vs. Frames. A full-size quilt may be quilted with good results in either a quilting hoop or a frame. Each has its special advantages. A hoop does not take much room while a quilt frame requires storage space when it's not in use. Hoop quilting allows you to turn the quilt in any direction for easy quilting while a quilt frame holds the quilt in a rigid position so that you have to move yourself rather than the quilt when the quilting turns in a new direction. Hoop quilting requires thorough basting of the quilt sandwich every 6″ in each direction, while use of a frame can sometimes eliminate basting altogether. Quilting in a hoop makes the project quite portable but only one person can work on the quilt at a time. Quilting in a frame means that the frame will probably have to stay in one place, but you can invite several friends to join you in working on the quilt.

Quilting in a Hoop. A quilting hoop may be round or oval, and it is much like an embroidery hoop only larger and heavier. Choose one that is at least 14″ but not much more than 18″ in diameter so that you will be able to comfortably reach to the center of it while quilting. Start quilting in the center of the quilt and work toward the outside edges. Position the inner hoop under the quilt where you intend to work. Unscrew the wing nut on the outer hoop to open fully, and place the outer hoop *over* the same spot on the quilt and gently ease it down over the other hoop and the quilt sandwich. Partially tighten the hardware; then check the underside to be sure that there are no wrinkles or puckers to interfere with the quilting before tightening the hardware to its final position. While quilting, you may find it helpful to prop the side of the hoop away from you on the edge of a table. As you finish quilting each area enclosed by the hoop, loosen and reposition it. When you reach the outside edges of the quilt, you may wish to baste a 6″ to 10″ band of scrap fabric or toweling to the quilt's edge so that you can maintain a firm tension in the hoop while quilting the outer edges.

Making a Frame. As a beginning quilter, you'll also want to try quilting in a floor frame. You might wish to borrow a ready-made frame to see how you like it, or you can make an inexpensive one by purchasing four pieces of standard 2x2 or 2x1 lumber stock and four C-clamps. You'll need two long boards (called the "rails" by quiltmakers), which are about nine feet long, and two boards (called "stretchers"), which are about three feet long. All of the boards should be sanded smooth. Cut two pieces of muslin the length of the long rails minus 6″ and about 10″ wide. Fold one piece of muslin in half lengthwise, and staple or tack its double-thickness raw edges along the length of a rail. Leave about 3″ of the board free at each end, and staple (with a staple gun) or tack (with carpet tacks and a hammer) every 2″ to 3″. Repeat for the other long rail.

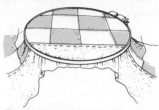

Baste scrap fabric to edge of quilt to maintain tension in hoop.

Staple muslin to rail.

Putting the Quilt in the Frame. Lay the rails along the two short (opposite) sides of the quilt sandwich and pin the lining and batting to the muslin strips with safety pins every three inches, or baste them securely. With the help of a friend, roll the quilt evenly onto one rail by turning the rail under the quilt until you reach about one foot from the quilt center. Repeat with the other rail so that a little more than two feet of the quilt's center section is left exposed. Place the three-foot lengths of lumber—the stretchers—at each end and attach them with C-clamps. Gently pull the unattached ends of the quilt taut by securing them with several cloth strips (cut approximately 2″ x 15″), which are wrapped around the stretchers and pinned to the quilt sandwich.

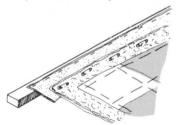

Pin quilt to muslin strips.

Attach stretchers with C-clamps; then secure quilt edges with cloth strips.

Using and Storing. This simple frame can be supported on the backs or arms of four chairs or by two sawhorses. The height of the frame will be determined by what seems comfortable to you while sitting in the chair that you plan to use. Once the center section of the quilt has been finished, the quilt may be rolled to one side or the other to expose a new section of the quilt to be quilted. When not working on the quilt, you can lean the frame against a wall out of the way. When the quilt is finished, the four boards and C-clamps can be disassembled and stored in a closet.

Lesson No. 22: How to Quilt

The quilting stitch is simple to do, and with a little practice you'll find that you are making your stitches even, straight, and small—just like the pros do it. You may wish to reread Lesson No. 7 (page 26) to remind yourself about the kind and color of thread to use when quilting as well as which size needle will work best.

Getting Started. Thread a needle with a single strand of thread that is about 20″ to 24″ long, and make a small knot with a 1″ to 1¼″ tail beyond it. Begin a line of quilting by inserting the needle into the top of the quilt about 1″ away from the place where the first stitch will be. Run the needle under the top and through some of the batting (but not into the lining), and bring the needle up at the spot where the first stitch begins. Pull the thread through, and give a gentle tug to pull the knot and tail through the top so they are buried in the batting.

Beginning a line of quilting: insert needle about an inch away from where the quilting will start. Bring thread through batting and up where first stitch begins.

Pop the knot through to inside of quilt so it doesn't show.

The Quilting Stitch. Whether or not you have used a thimble while piecing or appliquéing, you'll want to use one on the middle finger of your sewing hand while quilting. With the sewing hand above the quilt "sandwich" and the nonsewing hand underneath, insert the needle close to where the thread has come out—a scant ¹⁄₁₆″ (or smaller if you are able). The needle should go straight down, perpendicular to the surface of the quilt. Using the middle finger of your sewing hand (the one with the thimble on it), push the needle through until it lightly grazes the tip of the index finger on the nonsewing hand held against the underside of the quilt. Use the sewing-hand thumb (above the quilt) to gently depress the surface ahead of the planned stitch, and tip the eye of the needle down with the thimble to bring the point back up to the surface. The needle should now be flat against the quilt with the tip just showing on the surface. With a gentle rocking motion of the sewing hand, add two or three more stitches onto the needle; then push needle to the surface and pull the thread firmly but not too tight. Begin the next group of stitches with a new perpendicular thrust of the needle down through all quilt layers.

Beginning a quilting stitch: push the needle straight down through all quilt layers.

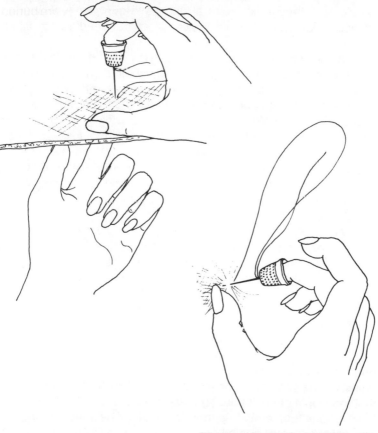

Tip the needle to complete the first quilting stitch.

When you first start to quilt, you'll want to experiment a bit with the position of the middle finger with the thimble on it. Some quiltmakers push the needle with the end of this thimble, keeping the thimble and needle aligned so that the needle is virtually an extension of the sewing finger. Others push the needle from the side of the thimble. Either position is fine, so you should choose whichever is more comfortable for you.

Also, you may find that taking just one stitch each time works best until you've had some practice. Concentrate on making evenly spaced stitches that are equal in length and go straight along the intended quilting line. As you practice, you'll find that your stitches become shorter and finer. Just be sure that the stitches on the lining side are as close as possible to the same length as the ones on the front, and that the thread has, in fact, gone through all three layers. An uninflated rubber balloon can be used to grasp the needle if it is hard to pull several stitches through several layers, although such a problem may indicate that your needle is tarnished and needs to be discarded.

Thread Tension. Practice will also tell you how much tension to put on the thread as you quilt. Pull each stitch (or group of stitches) on the needle through the quilt sandwich firmly but not so tight that the layers bunch up nor so loose that there are loops or gaps in the thread. Whenever possible, it is wise to stitch in a straight line for just a short distance—perhaps 6″ or less—and then turn in another direction. (If you quilt the whole 20″ of thread in one direction, later handling of the quilt will be more likely to add too much tension and break the thread; by changing directions every few inches, this kind of tension can be avoided.)

Avoiding Needle Pricks. The index finger that is under the quilt will be scratched over and over again by the needle's point coming down through the quilt sandwich. Some quiltmakers use a thimble on this finger to protect it while others hold a butter knife or spoon under the quilt to receive the prick of the needle coming through. Some wear a soft leather thimble or paint the tip of the finger with transparent nail polish. Some have mastered the technique of gently rolling the finger as the needle comes through to the lining side so that the needle's point merely grazes the finger rather than pricking it. Those quiltmakers who rely on their unprotected finger under the quilt usually build up a callous, which cushions the sting of the needle's point. If you decide that this last method works best for you, you may have to remove a few small blood stains from the fabric until your callous develops. A dab of cool (not hot) water or a bit of your own saliva will quickly remove such a stain.

Ending a Line of Quilting. There are two good ways to end a line of quilting. One method is to bring the needle up to the top surface just past the last stitch. Make a knot right against the fabric by bringing the needle under the thread where it comes out of the fabric and up through the loop it makes. Holding the thread close to that point, pull the loop tighter; then put your finger over the tightening loop and pull the last bit of thread to make the knot. Repeat the knot twice more to make a strong triple knot. Push the knot gently aside, and insert the needle into the hole where the thread came up. Run the needle along under the top and in the batting for about one inch or more, and then come back up to the surface (the needle should not go through the lining). Pull the thread taut and give it a gentle tug to pop the finishing knot under the quilt surface and into the batting. Check to be sure the knot (or thread) didn't go through to the lining side, and then clip the ending thread where it comes out on the front an inch away from the last quilting stitch.

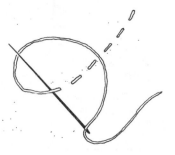

Make a knot by bringing the needle through the loop of thread.

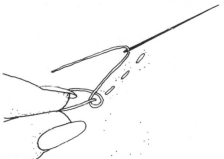

Hold onto the thread as you pull the loop tighter.

Insert the needle where the thread came up to pop the knot to the inside of the quilt.

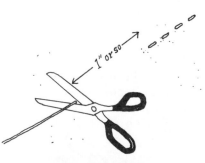

Finish with an inch-long stitch and clip thread at surface of quilt.

A second way to end a line of quilting does not use a knot, but your last stitch needs to be within an inch or less of a seam line. Push the needle down into the batting layer and not all the way through to the lining. Bring it back up against the nearest seam line. Either take a tiny backstitch in the seam where it will be hidden, or pull the thread away from the quilt top fabric so that you can slide

Take a stitch through the inside of the quilt and out at the seam line.

Take a small backstitch and bring the needle up an inch or so away along the seam.

If a backstitch can't be hidden, insert the needle into the hole where the thread came up.

Quilting stitches will be anchored by two inches of thread inside quilt.

the needle back down through the hole through which it just came. Bring the needle down through the quilt top and batting only, and then back to the top surface an inch or so away along the seam line. Clip the thread off at the surface. This will leave about two inches of thread inside of the quilt to anchor the stitching line.

You can end one row of quilting and begin another without stopping to cut the thread if the space between the two rows is an inch or less. Simply make a single, long stitch that goes through only the top layer and a little of the batting. Check the tension after making one more needleful of stitches to be sure that the long stitch hasn't been pulled too tightly or too loosely within the batting layer.

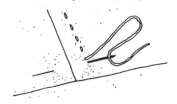

End one row of quilting and begin another by taking a long stitch inside the quilt.

What to Do About the Quilt Edges. When your quilting stitches approach the outside edges of the quilt, you will have to decide how and when to finish them. If your design flows out to the edge, you can quilt right into the seam allowance so that when the binding is put in place a few stitches will be covered by it. However, if your quilting design runs parallel to the edges and it would be noticeable if it doesn't line up evenly along the binding, you can stop quilting at the last border or an inch or so from the edges. Unthread the needle but do not cut the loose thread. Be sure that the edges are well basted and sew on the binding (see next page). Then go back and quilt the remaining small sections at the edge of the quilt.

Repairs. While you are quilting your quilt, you will be looking very closely at every inch of its surface, and this is probably the last time you will inspect it so carefully. If you see any loose seams, take the time to restitch them in matching thread so that the repair can't be seen. If there are raveling threads sticking up through a seam, clip them carefully close to the surface and work the ends back inside. If you find blood stains, pencil marks, or other discolorings, remove them carefully. If you find quilting knots that have popped back out to either surface, or loops of thread that didn't get pulled taut while quilting, work them back inside the quilt or redo a short section of quilting. If you promise yourself that you'll go back later to make repairs, you may not remember to do it, or you may not be able to find the spots that need repair. This is the time to take care of all of the little details that will make your finished quilt look its best.

Lesson No. 23: Binding the Quilt

When the quilting is finished, it is time to sew the binding in place around the edges of the quilt. The binding fabric may match the outermost border or it may contrast with that border while matching one of the other fabrics in the quilt top. It is usually made from the same cotton fabric as the rest of the quilt, and the quiltmaker may cut her own binding or use purchased binding that coordinates with the color scheme of the quilt. In the nineteenth century this binding was nearly always cut on the straight grain of the fabric, but many contemporary quiltmakers cut the binding on the bias.

Bias Binding. Purchased binding is usually made from bias strips, or you may cut your own from a length of yard goods. The longest unseamed piece of bias binding that can be cut from 44" fabric is about 62" long, and if you make continuous bias stripping from a square of fabric, many of the strips will be quite a bit shorter than 62" in length. Whether you use purchased bias binding or cut your own, several seams will appear at irregular intervals along the binding on the finished quilt.

A major advantage of bias binding is that it stretches easily and smoothly around any curved edges on a quilt border, but this same stretchiness requires careful handling to avoid ripples when the binding is attached. The back seam of the binding should lie directly behind the front one, and it should not shift or "crawl" in either direction because this is what causes an unattractive rippled look on a finished binding.

Straight-Grain Binding. Straight-grain binding does not stretch out of shape as easily as bias binding, so it has less tendency to cause ripples. Usually it is cut from a single piece of fabric that is as long as the side of the quilt plus a couple of inches for mitering the corners. This eliminates all seams in the binding except for the mitered corners, but it does require a lot of yardage to get the straight strips needed for the four sides of the quilt.

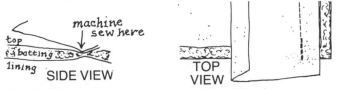

Single-layer binding: align edge of binding with edge of quilt top and stitch through all layers of quilt.

 *Fold binding to back, turn under seam allowance, and blindstitch by hand.*

Single Layer vs. Double. Binding may be used as a single or double layer. Single-layer binding is sewn to the front of the quilt through all three layers. Then it is folded around to the back, and the seam allowance is turned under before it is blindstitched in place. Single-layer binding makes the mitering of a corner much easier than double-layer binding because there are fewer layers of fabric in the miter.

Double-layer binding is folded in half lengthwise before it is sewn to the front side of the quilt through all three layers (top, batting, lining) with all raw edges matching. Then the folded edge is brought around to the back of the quilt and blindstitched in place. This folded edge is easy to sew along the seam line because you will not have to worry about turning under a raw edge evenly. The double layer also means that a worn outer layer may not have to be replaced as quickly as a single-layer binding, since batting will still be held inside by the inner layer of a double-layer binding.

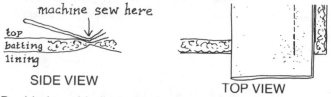

machine sew here

top
batting
lining

SIDE VIEW

TOP VIEW

Double-layer binding: align both raw edges of binding with edge of quilt top and stitch through all quilt layers.

hand sew here

Wrap double binding around to back of quilt and blindstitch folded edge of binding in place by hand.

Width of Binding. How wide should the binding be? A general rule of thumb is about 3/8" wide when finished. You may wish to make the binding a bit wider, but most quiltmakers prefer less than 3/4" in width for the binding. When you cut strips for the binding, you'll need to add the two 1/4" seam allowances and about 1/8" extra to allow for the front-to-back puffiness of the batting inside. If you will use single-layer binding, cut the strips twice the finished width plus 5/8". If you want double-layer binding, cut the strips four times the finished width plus 3/4".

Preparation. When you are ready to sew on the binding, be sure that quilting stitches or basting stitches hold all three layers of the quilt sandwich together at least as close as 1" from every border to be bound. If the actual binding will be about 3/8" wide—which is wider than the 1/4" seam allowance used in quiltmaking—you should measure and trim the batting and lining 3/8" outward from the seam line (not from the edge of the quilt). This will ensure that the finished binding will be well filled with batting and won't seem skimpy or flat.

Sewing the Binding. Pin the binding strip to the top side of the quilt sandwich with right sides together. Match the binding edge to the quilt-top edge with an extra inch or two of binding strip at each end of the quilt top. Sew through all layers—binding strip (either single or double layers), quilt top, batting, and lining—with a ¼" seam. (These seams that hold the binding to the front of the quilt will be strongest if you do them on the sewing machine.) First, on two opposite sides of the quilt, sew the seam from one end of the quilt top to the other right through the ¼" seam allowance and the extra lining and batting at each end. Then sew the binding onto the other two sides of the quilt by folding the already sewn bindings out of the way and ending the new seam just inside the already sewn binding (¼" from each edge). After sewing, be sure to inspect the entire distance of all seams to be sure that no accidental ripples or folds have been sewn into them. If there is a problem, rip out that part of the seam and fix it now—this is the only chance you'll have to create a perfectly smooth binding.

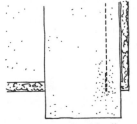

Sew two opposite binding strips clear to edge of quilt (including batting and lining).

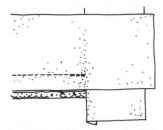

On other two sides of quilt, stitch only as far as seam of first binding strips.

Turn the quilt to the back, and pin the binding in place along the two opposite sides where the binding has been sewn all the way to each end of the quilt. If it is a single-layer binding, you'll need to turn under the ¼" seam allowance; if it is double-layer binding, you'll just be pinning the fold in place. Pin the entire length of each border to be sure that the binding is spaced evenly and does not ripple. Use a blind stitch just as you do in appliqué work to sew the binding in place. At each end, trim the binding to ¼" extra, tuck in the edges, and whipstitch a squared corner.

Fold the other two bindings to the back of the quilt, pin, and blindstitch in place. At each corner, take an extra stitch where this binding meets the one already sewn in place. Push the needle

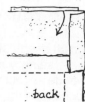

Trim end of single-layer binding strip and fold seam allowance to back.

Tuck under seam allowance along edge of binding strip and fold to back of quilt.

Blindstitch in place by hand.

through to the front side of the quilt exactly where the two bindings meet. On the front, trim the loose binding to about ¼" extra, and fold it on the diagonal to form a mitered corner. Blindstitch the diagonal fold in place on the front. Turn the quilt to the back side again. Tuck in the ends and blindstitch the fold in place, making either a butted corner or another mitered one.

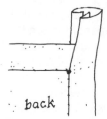

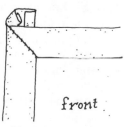

Fold other strip to back of quilt the same way and sew to corner of binding.

Trim strip; bring needle to front of quilt.

Tuck loose binding under to miter corner on front.

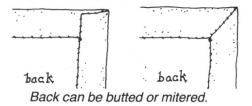

Back can be butted or mitered.

Lesson No. 24: Signing Your Quilt

A well-made quilt requires quite a bit of your time and effort, but when you finish the last stitch on the binding, you'll feel a great sense of accomplishment and much pride in your work. Whether you plan to give it as a gift, sell it on consignment, enter it in a quilt competition, or put it on your bed, it—and you—deserve one last finishing detail: a signature that tells everyone now and in the future that this is your quilt.

Information to Include. The minimal amount of information to include on your quilt is your full name and the year the quilt was made. It is also a good idea to document your city and state at the time the quilt was made. If you want to make it even easier for future generations to understand your work, you might identify the quilt's pattern, give a beginning and ending date for your work on the quilt, explain for whom it was made with the relationship to you, or describe the occasion for the gift. Some quilters also detail how many pieces are in the quilt top, how many hours they spent making it, how many spools of quilting thread they used, and so on.

Where to Sign. If you've taken a lot of time to make the quilt, it is worth taking a little more time to create a proper signature that cannot be lost or removed from the quilt. Although you can write the important information on a piece of paper, such documents have a tendency to get separated from a quilt, or they may deteriorate with time. Another method is to attach to the quilt a label with an embroidered, typewritten, or inked message. This will suffice in a pinch or may even be required by some competitions. But such labels can be easily detached from a quilt, and the information will be lost.

The best idea is to incorporate the important information about the quilt right into the quilt itself, either in the quilting design or with embroidery. Script or printing that is at least ½" tall will be easiest to quilt or embroider. The public library or needlework shops have books of lettering from which you can choose an alphabet, or you can letter the information in your own handwriting.

Quilting. For quilted signatures you may wish to make a stencil, or you can mark freehand in pencil. You can make the message very visible by quilting in light-colored thread on a dark fabric or vice versa. Or, you can make your message almost

Quilted signature.

invisible by quilting it in the same color of thread as the background fabric. A narrow inner or outer border might be the perfect place to quilt a long statement, or you can include shorter messages inside quilted motifs in a wide border or in a quilt block.

Embroidery. Embroidery is another way to make a permanent signature on your quilt. This may be done on the quilt top before the quilting, or you can do it later after the quilting is finished. You can sign on the front of the quilt as a part of the design, or you can place the signature on the back. You might choose a cross-stitched alphabet from a book. To do cross stitch, baste a piece of waste canvas (a special, fall-apart canvas available in needlework shops) in place, do the cross stitch over the canvas, moisten the canvas so that its starch dissolves, and then remove the canvas threads with a pair of tweezers.

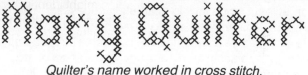

Quilter's name worked in cross stitch.

Another way to sign your quilt is to outline or chain stitch a signature created from a book's fancy lettering or your own freehand writing. If you prefer not to mark your quilt with a pencil for a freehand signature, use an indelible marking pen to write on a piece of white tissue paper (the kind that is used in gift boxes). Baste this tissue in place on the quilt, outline or chain stitch through tissue and quilt fabric, and then pull away the tissue paper with tweezers.

Embroidered signature done in outline stitch.

Why to Sign. Signing your quilt is just like an author putting his name on the cover of a book or an artist putting a signature on a canvas. Your quilt is your creative effort, and it should have a signature, too. Not only will it tell your contemporaries that you have made the quilt, but also it will identify you to future generations of your own family or to others doing research about quilts from this era.

Lesson No. 25: Caring for Your Quilt

Quilt care begins with the planned use of a quilt and the choice of materials for it. A wall quilt that will receive little wear and tear can be made from silks, satins, and other fragile fabrics, and it may have hand-sewn, narrow seams or delicate embroidery, beadwork, and other special effects. However, quilts that will be used on a bed need to be sturdy. They should be made from firm, colorfast, lightfast fabrics; stitched with strong thread; and well quilted with a bonded batting inside to prevent shifting or bearding. These characteristics will make a quilt stronger to begin with, and if the quilt needs to be cleaned, it will be better able to withstand such treatment.

Cleaning. The best cleaning method for quilts is no cleaning at all—or, at least, not until it is absolutely necessary. Then do the least amount of cleaning possible to maintain your quilts. Air them a couple of times a year by laying them out on a bed in a well-ventilated room, or by placing them face down on a sheet outdoors in the shade. If they have become dusty, a light vacuuming will be helpful. Do this by using the lowest suction level on your machine.

Dry cleaning is rarely recommended for a quilt because of the chemicals that may leave a residue in the fabrics and batting. Wet cleaning is an onerous job, both for the quilt and for the person(s) doing the cleaning. If the quilt is a utility quilt that requires frequent cleaning, you can risk putting it into a washing machine on the gentlest cycle with a mild detergent. You can also risk putting it into the dryer on the lowest (or no) heat cycle, although laying it out flat and face down on top of a sheet outdoors in the shade is probably preferable. (Never hang a wet quilt since its extra weight can easily break the quilting stitches or tear the fabrics.)

Sooner or later, laundering will begin to break down or fade the fabrics and threads used in a quilt just as the fabrics and threads in clothing, towels, and other bedding begin to deteriorate with continual machine washing. If your quilt is one that you care about a great deal, try to avoid this kind of cleaning. Take extra care of the quilt so that it doesn't get dirty, and if it does need cleaning, seek a professional to do wet cleaning by hand. You can ask at a museum or a quilt shop to find such assistance.

Light. A quilt used on a bed or wall should be protected from receiving too much light that can fade it. If possible, rotate the quilt on the bed each time that you remake it, and position the bed so that sunlight does not strike it. Hang a quilt only on walls that do not receive sunlight, and unless the quilt has an obvious top/bottom, rotate it on the wall every few months so that all parts of the quilt are equally exposed to any light sources. Even reflected light will eventually fade some fabrics, so close draperies during the day when the room is not in use.

Hanging. If you plan to hang a quilt on the wall, distribute its weight evenly. Sew a muslin sleeve all the way across the top of the quilt on the lining side. Slip a curtain rod, wooden dowel, or flat piece of wood through the sleeve, and suspend it at each end on brackets or other hangers. If the quilt is relatively small, you might consider using Velcro to attach it to a set of stretcher bars for hanging. Whenever possible, it is a good idea to have more than one quilt available for use on a particular wall. Not only will you be able to change the quilts to allow each to rest from being hung and from getting too much light, but also you'll be able to enjoy more than one piece of quilt art in that spot.

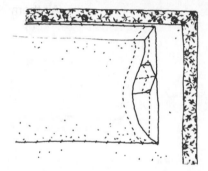

Sew a muslin sleeve to the quilt lining across the top of the quilt.

Insert a dowel, curtain rod, or flat piece of wood through the sleeve to hang the quilt.

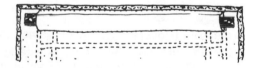

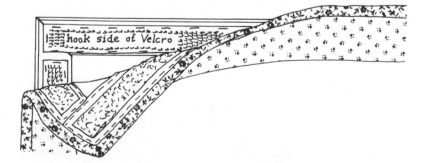

A small quilt can be hung with Velcro on stretcher bars.

Storing. A little bit of care and planning is needed when storing quilts, too. Find a place that is away from light, moderate in temperature (not a hot attic nor a cold basement), well ventilated, dry, and clean. Plastic bags hold in moisture and pests, allowing mildew or other damage to occur, so never use such bags for quilt storage. Instead, wrap the quilt in a clean cotton sheet or pillowcase, or store it in an acid-free box (available from museums, some quilt shops, and mail-order sources). When folding a quilt for storage, fold it right sides in with as few folds as possible. Acid-free paper crumpled into long rolls and placed in the folds will help to keep creases from becoming permanent, and refolding the quilt on different fold lines every few months will also minimize damage. Unless quilts can be stored singly in boxes, they should not be stacked more than two deep because the added weight will also create damaging pressure on the fibers.

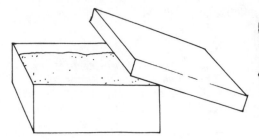

Use acid-free boxes or cotton sheets and pillowcases, rather than plastic bags, for storing quilts.

Cushion the folds with acid-free paper to help prevent creasing.

Quilts would probably last forever if they were laid out singly, without folding, on a flat surface in a darkened room that was well-ventilated, had a relative humidity of about 50%, and was free from pollution, dust, mold, insects, rodents, and so on. But most of us make quilts so that they can be seen and used and enjoyed, and this means that optimum conditions for their survival will not be possible. However, a bit of common sense about caring for them and using them will ensure that they give us pleasure for a long time—if not forever.

SUGGESTED READING

Jinny Beyer, *The Quilter's Album of Blocks and Borders* (1980, EPM Publications, Inc.). 750 quilt patterns with easy drafting instructions and border plans.

Michael James, *The Quiltmaker's Handbook* (1978) and *The 2nd Quiltmaker's Handbook: Creative Approaches to Contemporary Quilt Design* (1981, Prentice-Hall, Inc.). One of America's contemporary quiltmakers explains his techniques for designing and quilting.

Bonnie Leman and Judy Martin, *Taking the Math Out of Making Patchwork Quilts* (1981, Moon Over the Mountain Publishing Co.). Charts and handy references on all aspects of measuring and calculating for quiltmaking.

Bonnie Leman, Marie Shirer, and Susie Ennis, *Patchwork Sampler Legacy Quilt: Intermediate and Advanced Lessons in Patchwork* (1976, Rev. Ed. 1984, Leman Publications, Inc.). A sequel to this book for beginners with twelve patterns in two sizes that teach advanced quiltmaking techniques.

Judy Martin, *Judy Martin's Ultimate Book of Quilt Block Patterns* (1988, Crosley-Griffith Publishing Company). 174 quilt blocks shown in color with piecing diagrams, yardage charts, full-sized quilting motifs and patterns.

Susan Richardson McKelvey, *Light & Shadows: Optical Illusion in Quilts* (1989, C & T Publishing). Intensive look at ways to make color, perspective, and transparency work in fabric and thread with projects to help you develop skills in these areas.

Nancy O'Bryant Puentes, *First Aid for Family Quilts* (1986, Moon Over the Mountain Publishing Co.). Describes practices for cleaning, storing, and protecting quilts.

Marie Shirer, *Quilt Settings—A Workbook* (1989, Moon Over The Mountain Publishing Company). Shows how to combine many settings and block patterns in numerous ways to create original quilts.

Pattern for Cover Quilt (Daisy Chain)

Quilt Size: 80" x 95"; **Block Size:** 7½" (set 9x11, 3 borders)

Yardage (44" fabric): From 4¼ yds. muslin cut 2 strips 1¾" x 87"; 2 strips 1¾" x 72"; 49 B, 50 E, and 200 D. From 3 yds. red solid cut 2 strips 3" x 99"; 2 strips 3" x 84"; binding 10 yds. x 1½"; 200 C and 200 Cr. From 1⅜ yds. light scraps cut 328 A. From 2⅛ yds. dark scraps cut 524 A. Also needed are 5½ yds. for lining (with one vertical seam) and batting 84" x 99".

Assembly: Sew a dark A to each of four long sides of muslin B. Repeat to make 49 Y blocks.

Sew a light A to a dark A to form a square Unit 1. Repeat three times. Sew a red C to one side of muslin D and a red Cr to the other side of D to form square as in Unit 2. Repeat three times. See Fig. 1 below. Sew a Unit 2 between two Unit 1's. Repeat. Sew the two remaining Unit 2 squares to opposite sides of a muslin E. Sew the three segments together as shown to complete Block Z. Repeat to make 50 Z blocks.

Sew five Z blocks alternately with four Y blocks to make a row. Repeat to make six rows like this. Sew five Y blocks alternately with four Z blocks to make a row. Repeat to make five rows like this. Sew the rows together, alternating rows starting with Block Y and rows starting with Block Z.

Add muslin borders, mitering corners and trimming excess from seam allowances. To make pieced borders, sew a dark A to a light A to form a square. Repeat to make 128 squares. Sew squares in rows as shown, and add to top, bottom, and sides of quilt. Add red borders, mitering corners.

Mark quilting pattern of your choice in octagons. Quilt as marked, outline quilt all patches, and bind in red to finish.

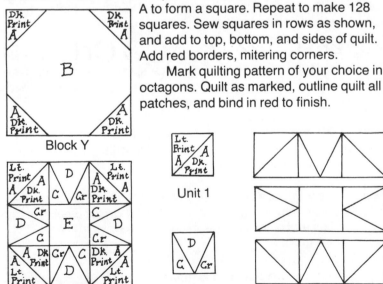

Block Y

Block Z

Unit 1

Unit 2

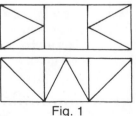

Fig. 1

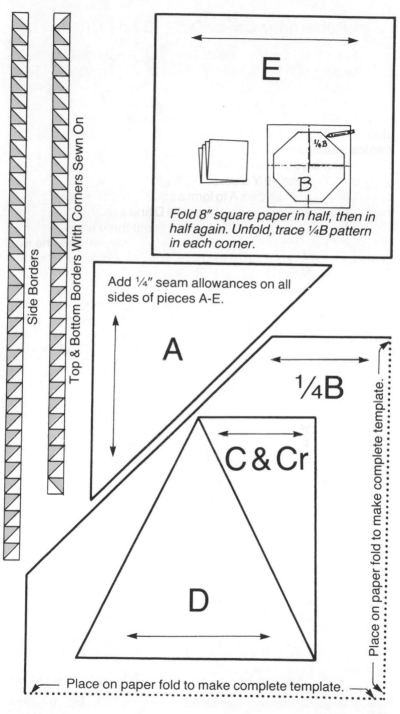

Side Borders

Top & Bottom Borders With Corners Sewn On

E

Fold 8″ square paper in half, then in half again. Unfold, trace ¼B pattern in each corner.

¼B

B

Add ¼″ seam allowances on all sides of pieces A-E.

A

C & Cr

D

Place on paper fold to make complete template.

Place on paper fold to make complete template.

NOTES